CHRIS DEVON

# API Development Essentials with Flask

# Contents

# Introduction to Flask and APIs

F lask is a micro web framework written in Python, designed to be lightweight and flexible, making it a popular choice for developers looking to build web applications or APIs. It emphasizes simplicity, offering an unopinionated and modular approach to development. With Flask, developers have the freedom to choose the tools, libraries, and components that best fit their needs. This flexibility is one of the core reasons why Flask is widely used in creating APIs, especially when the goal is to build something scalable, easy to maintain, and fast to develop.

What is Flask?

Flask was created by Armin Ronacher in 2010 as an alternative to larger, more rigid frameworks like Django. It is built on top of the **Werkzeug** toolkit and **Jinja2**, a powerful templating engine, both of which add to Flask's functionality without forcing developers into a specific development pattern.

Flask is often referred to as a "micro" framework. This doesn't mean it lacks features; rather, it means Flask keeps the core minimal, allowing developers to add only what they need. It's like starting with a blank canvas where you have the freedom to decide which features to implement, whether that's form validation, user authentication, or database integration. You choose what to add, rather than having the framework dictate the architecture of your project.

Some of the key advantages of Flask include:

- **Minimalism and Simplicity**: It doesn't come with pre-set features or functionalities, making it perfect for small applications, prototypes, or when developers want complete control over the application's structure.

- **Extensibility**: Although the core is minimal, Flask has a rich ecosystem of extensions that can be added as needed. These extensions are easy to plug in and provide functionalities like database integration, authentication, or API documentation.
- **Flexibility**: You're free to structure your project however you like. Whether you're building a small app or something larger, Flask gives you room to expand and adapt.

Flask is often the framework of choice for developers looking to get up and running quickly without being forced into using particular tools or libraries. It provides everything necessary to build a fully functional API without overwhelming the developer.

Understanding APIs

APIs, or **Application Programming Interfaces**, serve as a bridge between different software systems, allowing them to communicate with each other. They are the backbone of modern web development, enabling applications to share data and functionality. APIs can be thought of as the connectors that allow different pieces of software to work together, whether within a single application or between two separate services.

In the context of web development, APIs are primarily used to allow different applications (or parts of the same application) to talk to each other over the internet. For example, a mobile app might use an API to communicate with a server and retrieve user data, or a weather application might use an external API to get real-time weather information.

There are several types of APIs, with **REST (Representational State Transfer)** being one of the most widely used for web applications. RESTful APIs, which follow a set of principles such as statelessness and a uniform interface, have become the standard due to their simplicity and scalability.

REST API Basics

A REST API is an architectural style, not a standard or protocol, that defines a set of constraints for creating web services. These constraints promote scalability and separation of concerns. REST APIs work with standard HTTP methods (GET, POST, PUT, DELETE) and use resources (typically represented as URLs) to perform CRUD operations (Create, Read, Update, Delete).

The key principles of REST are:

- **Statelessness**: Each API request should contain all the information the server needs to fulfill it. The server should not store any client state between requests.
- **Client-Server Architecture**: The client and server should be independent of each other. The client is responsible for handling the presentation of data, while the server handles the business logic and data storage.
- **Uniform Interface**: The API should provide a consistent and uniform way of accessing resources.
- **Resource-Based URLs**: Resources (like users, products, or posts) are represented by URIs (Uniform Resource Identifiers). For example, /users might represent the collection of all users, while /users/123 might represent a specific user with the ID of 123.

Understanding these basic principles of REST APIs is crucial as it sets the foundation for API development in Flask.

Why Flask for API Development?

Flask is a perfect fit for API development for a number of reasons:

1. **Lightweight Framework**: Flask is known for its minimalistic nature. Unlike larger frameworks like Django, which come with many built-in features, Flask allows developers to pick and choose exactly what they need. For API development, this is particularly important because it allows developers to focus solely on the API without worrying about unnecessary overhead.

2. **Modular Approach**: Flask's modularity means you can easily add functionality as needed. For example, you can start with a simple API and then add user authentication, request validation, or database access as the project grows.

3. **Rich Ecosystem of Extensions**: Flask has a robust ecosystem of extensions that can be easily integrated into an API project. Extensions like **Flask-RESTful** simplify the creation of RESTful APIs, while **Flask-SQLAlchemy** provides seamless database integration.

4. **Ease of Learning**: Flask is known for being beginner-friendly, making it a great option for developers who are just starting out with API development. Its simple, intuitive syntax is easy to pick up, while the framework's flexibility and scalability mean that even experienced developers can use it to build large, complex APIs.

5. **Great Documentation and Community Support**: Flask's documentation is clear and comprehensive, making it easy to find answers to common questions. Additionally, Flask has a large, active community of developers who contribute to its ecosystem and provide support through forums and tutorials.

6. **Scalability**: While Flask is lightweight and minimalistic, it can scale to handle large projects. By using a microservices architecture, developers can break down larger applications into smaller, independent services, each with its own API built with Flask. This makes Flask a good choice for both small and large-scale API projects.

The Role of APIs in Modern Web Development

APIs have become an essential part of modern web development. They allow different systems to communicate with one another and share data and functionality. Whether it's enabling mobile apps to interact with a backend, allowing third-party services to integrate with an application, or providing the infrastructure for microservices, APIs are the glue that holds much of the modern web together.

One of the primary benefits of APIs is that they allow for the separation of concerns. For example, a frontend web application can focus solely on user interaction and presentation, while the backend API handles data storage, business logic, and other server-side operations. This separation makes it easier to maintain and scale both the frontend and backend independently.

Moreover, APIs have enabled the rise of third-party services and integrations. A company can build its own API to allow other developers to integrate with their services. This has led to the creation of ecosystems around popular APIs like those provided by Twitter, Google, and Stripe, enabling developers to build innovative applications that leverage these services.

APIs are also crucial for mobile development, as mobile apps rely heavily on APIs to communicate with backend services. Without APIs, mobile apps would be unable to send or receive data, rendering them unable to function in any meaningful way.

Flask vs. Other Web Frameworks for APIs

Flask is not the only Python web framework that can be used for API development. **Django**, for example, is another popular framework that comes with a lot of built-in functionality. However, there are some key differences between Flask and Django that make Flask a better fit for certain types of projects, especially APIs.

1. **Flexibility vs. Convention**: Django is often described as a "batteries-included" framework, meaning it comes with a lot of built-in functionality, such as an admin panel, ORM, and form validation. This is great for developers who want to quickly get up and running with a full-featured web application. However, this also means that developers are constrained by Django's conventions. Flask, on the other hand, offers more flexibility, allowing developers to use only the tools they need and build their application from the ground up.

2. **Simplicity for API Development**: Django's features are great for building large web applications, but they can add unnecessary complexity when building a simple API. Flask's minimalist nature makes it easier to create an API without having to worry about additional features that aren't necessary for the project.

3. **Performance**: Flask is lightweight, which often leads to better performance for API applications, especially when compared to more feature-rich frameworks like Django. While Flask and Django are both capable of handling large-scale applications, Flask's lower overhead can result in better performance for APIs.

4. **Learning Curve**: Flask's simplicity and minimalism mean that it has a gentler learning curve than Django. This makes Flask a great choice for developers who are new to web development or API creation.

5. **Scalability**: While Django is often seen as the go-to framework for large applications, Flask's flexibility makes it equally capable of handling large-scale projects, particularly when it comes to microservices architectures. Flask's ability to integrate with tools like Docker and Kubernetes also makes it easy to scale applications as needed.

Summary

Flask is a powerful and flexible framework for building APIs. Its lightweight, unopinionated nature makes it a great choice for developers who want full control over their applications without being forced into a particular architecture. APIs themselves are crucial for modern web development, enabling different systems to communicate and share data seamlessly.

In this book, we will explore how to leverage Flask's flexibility to build efficient, scalable APIs, covering everything from the basics of setting up a Flask environment to more advanced topics like authentication, asynchronous programming, and deployment. With Flask, you'll have the tools you need to build APIs that power modern web and mobile applications, whether you're working on a small project or building a large, scalable system.

This chapter lays the groundwork for the rest of the book, providing an understanding of Flask's strengths and how APIs fit into the broader world of web development. Next, we'll dive into setting up your Flask development environment, where you'll begin your hands-on journey into API development.

# Setting Up Your Development Environment

A well-prepared development environment is crucial for a smooth and efficient workflow when building APIs with Flask. In this chapter, we'll guide you through setting up your environment for Flask development, ensuring that your tools and dependencies are configured correctly. Whether you're working on a Windows, macOS, or Linux system, you'll learn how to set up Flask, use virtual environments to manage dependencies, and structure your project for maximum productivity.

Installing Flask

The first step in Flask development is to install Flask itself. Flask runs on Python, so you'll need Python installed on your system. Flask is compatible with both Python 2.x and Python 3.x, but for long-term support and access to the latest features, we recommend using Python 3.x.

Installing Python

If Python isn't already installed on your system, follow the steps below to install it:

**Windows**:

- Download the latest version of Python from the official Python website. During installation, make sure to check the box that says **"Add Python**

**to PATH**". This will make it easier to run Python from the command line. Once installed, verify the installation by running python —version in your command prompt or terminal.

**macOS**:

- macOS typically comes with Python pre-installed, but it may not be the latest version. You can install the latest version of Python using Homebrew, a popular package manager for macOS. Run the following commands to install Homebrew (if you don't have it) and then install Python:

```
/bin/bash -c "$(curl -fsSL
https://raw.githubusercontent.com/Homebrew/install/HEAD/install.sh)"
brew install python
```

**Linux**:

- Most Linux distributions come with Python pre-installed. You can check your version by running:

```
python3 --version
```

- If Python 3 is not installed, use your distribution's package manager to install it. For example, on Ubuntu, you can run:

```
sudo apt update
sudo apt install python3
```

Once Python is installed, we can move on to installing Flask.

Installing Flask via pip

Once you have Python installed, the next step is to install Flask. Flask is available on **PyPI** (the Python Package Index), which makes it easy to install using Python's package manager, pip. The process is straightforward.

First, open your terminal (or command prompt on Windows) and install Flask with the following command:

```
pip install Flask
```

To verify that Flask is installed, you can check the installed version:

```
flask --version
```

If Flask is installed correctly, you should see the version number displayed.

Creating and Managing Virtual Environments

When working on Python projects, it's good practice to use **virtual environments**. A virtual environment is an isolated Python environment that ensures your project dependencies don't interfere with other Python projects or system-wide packages.

Virtual environments allow you to install project-specific libraries without affecting the global Python installation on your system. This is particularly important when working with multiple projects that may require different versions of the same libraries.

Setting Up a Virtual Environment

Python 3 includes a built-in module for creating virtual environments, called venv. Here's how to set it up:

**Windows**:

- Open your command prompt.
- Navigate to your project directory:

```
cd path\to\your\project
```

- Create a virtual environment by running:

```
python -m venv venv
```

This will create a directory called venv in your project folder, which contains the isolated Python environment.

- To activate the virtual environment, use the following command:

```
venv\Scripts\activate
```

You should see (venv) at the beginning of your command prompt, indicating that the virtual environment is active.

**macOS/Linux**:

- Open your terminal.
- Navigate to your project directory:

```
cd path/to/your/project
```

- Create a virtual environment with:

```
python3 -m venv venv
```

- Activate the virtual environment with:

```
source venv/bin/activate
```

Once the virtual environment is activated, you can install Flask within this isolated environment. You can confirm Flask is installed within the virtual environment by running:

```
pip install Flask
```

From now on, when you run your project or install additional libraries, the virtual environment will ensure they remain separate from your global Python installation.

Deactivating the Virtual Environment

When you're done working on the project, you can deactivate the virtual environment by simply running the following command:

```
deactivate
```

This will return you to the global Python environment. When you come back to work on the project, don't forget to reactivate the virtual environment using the commands mentioned earlier.

Installing Flask Extensions

While Flask is minimalistic by design, it has a rich ecosystem of extensions that can be easily added to your project. Flask extensions add extra functionality to the framework without compromising its simplicity. For API development, several extensions will be helpful, such as Flask-RESTful, Flask-SQLAlchemy, and Flask-JWT-Extended.

Let's take a look at how to install these extensions:

Flask-RESTful

Flask-RESTful is an extension for building RESTful APIs with Flask. It adds powerful abstractions and tools for developing APIs more efficiently. To install it, run:

```
pip install Flask-RESTful
```

Flask-SQLAlchemy

Flask-SQLAlchemy simplifies database integration with Flask. It provides an ORM (Object Relational Mapping) that allows developers to interact with databases using Python objects. You can install it with:

```
pip install Flask-SQLAlchemy
```

Flask-JWT-Extended

Flask-JWT-Extended allows you to easily integrate JSON Web Tokens (JWTs) for securing your API endpoints. To install it, run:

```
pip install Flask-JWT-Extended
```

You can also explore other useful extensions based on the needs of your API, such as Flask-Migrate (for database migrations) and Flask-Swagger (for API documentation).

Structuring Your Flask Project

Flask gives developers the freedom to structure their projects in various ways, making it flexible for both small and large applications. However, following a clear, scalable structure from the start will make your project easier to maintain and scale as it grows.

Simple Structure for Small Projects

For small projects or when you're just starting, a simple project structure may look like this:

```
/my-flask-app
    /static
    /templates
    app.py
    config.py
    requirements.txt
    README.md
```

- **app.py**: The main file where your Flask application and routes are defined.
- **config.py**: Configuration settings for the application, such as database connection strings or secret keys.
- **/static**: A folder to store static files like CSS, JavaScript, or images.
- **/templates**: A folder to store HTML files (if your application includes any frontend components).
- **requirements.txt**: A file listing the dependencies for your project. This is generated by running:

```
pip freeze > requirements.txt
```

- The requirements.txt file helps other developers (or yourself on a different machine) install the correct versions of your project's dependencies.

Modular Structure for Larger Projects

For larger applications, it's best to break your code into modules and packages. This makes your code more organized and scalable. A more complex structure might look like this:

```
/my-flask-app
    /app
        /models
        /routes
        /static
        /templates
        __init__.py
        config.py
    /tests
    run.py
    requirements.txt
    README.md
```

- **/app**: Contains the main application code.
- **/init.py**: This file initializes the Flask application. It imports the necessary extensions and registers blueprints (modular components of your app).
- **/models**: Contains database models (if you're using a database).
- **/routes**: Contains the route definitions for your API.
- **/static**: Stores static files.
- **/templates**: Stores HTML templates (if used).
- **config.py**: Configuration settings for different environments (development, testing, production).
- **/tests**: Contains unit tests for the application.
- **run.py**: This file is used to run the Flask application. It imports the Flask instance from app/__init__.py and runs the app.

Using Blueprints for Modular Development

As your application grows, you'll want to organize different parts of your API into modules. Flask provides a feature called **blueprints**, which allow you to organize your routes and functionality into separate components that can be easily managed.

For example, if you're building an API for an e-commerce site, you might have separate blueprints for handling user accounts, product catalogs, and orders:

```
/app
    /users
        __init__.py
        routes.py
        models.py
    /products
        __init__.py
        routes.py
        models.py
    /orders
        __init__.py
        routes.py
        models.py
```

Each module has its own routes.py file, where you define the routes related to that module, and its own models.py for the data models.

In your __init__.py file, you would register each blueprint with the main Flask app like this:

```
from flask import Flask
from app.users.routes import users
from app.products.routes import products
from app.orders.routes import orders

app = Flask(__name__)

app.register_blueprint(users)
app.register_blueprint(products)
app.register_blueprint(orders)
```

This modular approach ensures that as your application grows, you can maintain a clean, organized structure that makes it easy to add new features or update existing ones.

Setting Up Version Control with Git

Once your project is set up, it's important to track your code changes with version control. **Git** is the most widely used version control system, and it integrates seamlessly with platforms like GitHub, GitLab, or Bitbucket.

To get started with Git:

- **Initialize Git in your project folder**:

```
git init
```

- **Create a .gitignore file** to exclude unnecessary files (like virtual environments or compiled files):

```
venv/
__pycache__/
*.pyc
```

- **Commit your changes**:

```
git add .
git commit -m "Initial commit"
```

- **Push your code to a remote repository**, like GitHub:

```
git remote add origin <your-repository-url>
git push -u origin master
```

Version control allows you to collaborate with others, keep track of code changes, and roll back to previous versions if needed.

# Building Your First API with Flask

Now that you've set up your development environment, it's time to dive into building your first API with Flask. This chapter will walk you through creating a basic API that interacts with users, handling different HTTP methods, and returning JSON responses. By the end of this chapter, you'll have a solid understanding of how to build foundational APIs using Flask.

Understanding Flask Routing

Routing is one of the core concepts in Flask. It refers to how URL paths are mapped to specific pieces of code, called view functions. Each route corresponds to a specific function that processes requests made to a particular endpoint.

In Flask, you define routes using the @app.route decorator. This decorator binds a URL to a function, so when a user accesses a specific URL, Flask knows which function to execute.

Example of a Basic Route

Let's start by creating a basic Flask application with a simple route. In your project folder, create a file named app.py and add the following code:

```
from flask import Flask

app = Flask(__name__)

@app.route('/')
```

```
def home():
    return "Welcome to your first Flask API!"

if __name__ == '__main__':
    app.run(debug=True)
```

## Breakdown of the Code

- **Importing Flask**: The first line imports the Flask class from the flask package.
- **Creating a Flask Instance**: We create an instance of the Flask class, passing __name__ as an argument. This is the name of the application's module or package, which helps Flask locate resources and templates.
- **Defining a Route**: The @app.route('/') line is a decorator that tells Flask to execute the home function when a user visits the root URL (/). This function simply returns a welcome message.
- **Running the App**: Finally, the if __name__ == '__main__' block ensures that the app runs only if the script is executed directly (and not imported as a module).

To run this app, activate your virtual environment and run:

```
python app.py
```

This will start a local development server, and you can visit http://127.0.0.1: 5000/ in your browser to see your first Flask route in action.

## Handling HTTP Methods

In the example above, the route only responds to GET requests by default. However, a full-fledged API should be able to handle various HTTP methods like GET, POST, PUT, and DELETE to perform different actions. Flask makes this easy by allowing you to specify which methods a route should accept.

Example: Handling Different Methods

Let's extend the previous example to create an API that handles different methods. Update your app.py file as follows:

```python
from flask import Flask, request, jsonify

app = Flask(__name__)

users = [
    {"id": 1, "name": "Alice"},
    {"id": 2, "name": "Bob"}
]

@app.route('/users', methods=['GET'])
def get_users():
    return jsonify(users)

@app.route('/users', methods=['POST'])
def add_user():
    new_user = request.get_json()
    new_user['id'] = len(users) + 1
    users.append(new_user)
    return jsonify(new_user), 201

@app.route('/users/<int:user_id>', methods=['PUT'])
def update_user(user_id):
    for user in users:
        if user['id'] == user_id:
            user.update(request.get_json())
            return jsonify(user)
    return jsonify({"error": "User not found"}), 404

@app.route('/users/<int:user_id>', methods=['DELETE'])
def delete_user(user_id):
    global users
    users = [user for user in users if user['id'] != user_id]
    return jsonify({"message": "User deleted"})

if __name__ == '__main__':
```

```
app.run(debug=True)
```

Breakdown of the Code

- **Importing Additional Modules**: We've imported request and jsonify from Flask. request allows us to access incoming request data, while jsonify makes it easy to return JSON responses.
- **In-Memory Data Storage**: We've created a list called users to store user data in memory. In a real-world scenario, you would connect this to a database.
- **Handling GET Requests**: The /users route with the GET method returns a JSON representation of the users list.
- **Handling POST Requests**: The /users route with the POST method accepts a JSON payload containing new user data. It then appends the new user to the list and returns the new user object with a 201 (Created) status code.
- **Handling PUT Requests**: The /users/<int:user_id> route with the PUT method accepts a user ID as part of the URL. It updates the user data if the user ID matches an existing user, or returns a 404 error if not found.
- **Handling DELETE Requests**: The /users/<int:user_id> route with the DELETE method removes the specified user from the list.

Testing the API Endpoints

To test the API endpoints, you can use a tool like **Postman** or **cURL**. Postman provides an easy-to-use interface for sending HTTP requests to your API and inspecting the responses.

**GET** /users:

Make a GET request to http://127.0.0.1:5000/users. You should receive a list of users in the response.

**POST** /users:

Make a POST request to http://127.0.0.1:5000/users with a JSON body like:

21

```
{
    "name": "Charlie"
}
```

This should add a new user and return the user object in the response.

**PUT** /users/3:

Make a PUT request to http://127.0.0.1:5000/users/3 with a JSON body like:

```
{
    "name": "Charlie Brown"
}
```

This should update the user with ID 3.

**DELETE** /users/3:

Make a DELETE request to http://127.0.0.1:5000/users/3. This should remove the user with ID 3 from the list.

Returning JSON Responses

APIs typically communicate using **JSON (JavaScript Object Notation)**, a lightweight data format that is easy to read and write. In the examples above, we used jsonify to return JSON responses. jsonify automatically converts Python dictionaries to JSON format and sets the appropriate content type for the response.

For example, the following line:

```
return jsonify(users)
```

Converts the users list into JSON and returns it to the client. Flask takes care of setting the **Content-Type** header to application/json.

Debugging Common Issues

Building APIs with Flask can sometimes lead to unexpected errors. Fortunately, Flask comes with a built-in debugger that helps you identify and resolve issues quickly. Here are some common issues you might encounter and tips for debugging them:

- **Incorrect Route Names**: If you're not seeing the response you expect, check that the route in your URL matches the route definition in your code. Flask routes are case-sensitive, so a mismatch in case can lead to 404 errors.
- **Missing or Incorrect HTTP Methods**: If your route doesn't respond to a particular method, check that you've specified the correct methods in your route definition. For example:

```
@app.route('/example', methods=['GET', 'POST'])
```

- **Incorrect JSON Structure**: When sending JSON data to your API, ensure that the structure matches what your view function expects. If you're using Postman, you can select the "**JSON**" format to avoid syntax errors in your payload.

To enable Flask's built-in debugger, set the debug parameter to True when calling app.run():

```
if __name__ == '__main__':
    app.run(debug=True)
```

With debugging enabled, Flask will provide detailed error messages and a stack trace in the browser whenever an error occurs. This makes it easier to identify the root cause of an issue.

Organizing Your Code for Scalability

As your application grows, the number of routes and the amount of code in your main file (app.py) can become overwhelming. To maintain a clean and scalable codebase, it's a good idea to break your code into separate modules and use **blueprints**.

**Blueprints** allow you to group related routes together, making your code more organized and modular. Let's refactor the app.py code using blueprints.

Refactoring with Blueprints

**Create a new folder named users** in your project directory. Inside this folder, create the following files:

- __init__.py
- routes.py

**Move the routes to routes.py**:

```python
from flask import Blueprint, request, jsonify

users = Blueprint('users', __name__)

user_data = [
    {"id": 1, "name": "Alice"},
    {"id": 2, "name": "Bob"}
]

@users.route('/users', methods=['GET'])
def get_users():
    return jsonify(user_data)

@users.route('/users', methods=['POST'])
def add_user():
    new_user = request.get_json()
    new_user['id'] = len(user_data) + 1
    user_data.append(new_user)
    return jsonify(new_user), 201

@users.route('/users/<int:user_id>', methods=['PUT'])
```

```
def update_user(user_id):
    for user in user_data:
        if user['id'] == user_id:
            user.update(request.get_json())
            return jsonify(user)
    return jsonify({"error": "User not found"}), 404

@users.route('/users/<int:user_id>', methods=['DELETE'])
def delete_user(user_id):
    global user_data
    user_data = [user for user in user_data if user['id'] !=
    user_id]
    return jsonify({"message": "User deleted"})
```

**Update app.py** to register the blueprint:

```
from flask import Flask
from users.routes import users

app = Flask(__name__)
app.register_blueprint(users)

if __name__ == '__main__':
    app.run(debug=True)
```

By using blueprints, you can organize related routes into separate modules. This makes your project easier to maintain, especially as it grows larger and more complex.

# RESTful API Design Principles

Building a RESTful API involves more than just writing code—it's about adhering to a set of principles and best practices that allow for scalable, maintainable, and user-friendly applications. REST (Representational State Transfer) is not a standard but an architectural style that defines how web services should behave. In this chapter, you'll learn about RESTful principles, resource-based design, and how to effectively apply them in Flask to create clean and efficient APIs.

What Makes an API RESTful?

REST, introduced by Roy Fielding in his doctoral dissertation, is built on a set of six architectural constraints. Adhering to these constraints is what makes an API truly RESTful:

1. **Client-Server Architecture**: The client and server should be separate entities, each with a well-defined responsibility. The server provides resources, and the client consumes them. This separation allows the client and server to be developed, maintained, and scaled independently.
2. **Statelessness**: Each request from the client to the server must contain all the information needed to process the request. The server should not store any session-related information between requests. This ensures that each request is independent, which simplifies scalability.
3. **Cacheability**: Responses from the server must be explicitly labeled as cacheable or non-cacheable. This allows clients to cache responses, improving performance by reducing the number of requests to the

server.

4. **Uniform Interface**: REST APIs should have a consistent and standard-ized way of interacting with resources. This includes the use of standard HTTP methods (GET, POST, PUT, DELETE), consistent URIs, and clear representations of resources.

5. **Layered System**: A RESTful API should be designed in layers, where each layer has its own responsibility. For example, a layer may handle security, while another handles data storage. This allows for modular development and simplifies the maintenance of complex systems.

6. **Code on Demand (Optional)**: Although not always necessary, REST allows the server to extend client functionality by sending executable code (like JavaScript) to the client. This is optional and is often not used in typical API scenarios.

By adhering to these principles, RESTful APIs provide a clear and consistent way of interacting with resources, making them easy to understand, consume, and scale.

Designing Resource Models

In REST, resources are the key entities that the API manages. Resources can represent users, products, orders, or any other entities in your application. Each resource should be represented as a **noun** and have a **unique identifier**.

Resource Identification with URIs

A resource in a RESTful API is identified by a URI (Uniform Resource Identifier). Let's take the example of a user management system. Here's how you might represent different resources and actions:

- **Resource**: Users
- **Endpoint**: /users

**Example URIs**:

- **GET** /users: Fetch a list of users.

- **POST** /users: Create a new user.
- **GET** /users/{id}: Fetch a specific user by their ID.
- **PUT** /users/{id}: Update an existing user by their ID.
- **DELETE** /users/{id}: Delete a user by their ID.

The key idea here is that each resource (like users) has a unique URL that represents it. Actions like fetching, creating, updating, and deleting are represented by the HTTP methods used with these URLs.

Using HTTP Methods Correctly

One of the core principles of RESTful API design is the proper use of HTTP methods. Each method has a specific purpose and meaning:

- **GET**: Used to fetch or retrieve resources. GET requests are idempotent and should not modify any server-side data.
- **POST**: Used to create new resources. POST requests should include the data for the new resource in the request body.
- **PUT**: Used to update existing resources. PUT requests should include the complete updated resource in the request body.
- **PATCH**: Used to partially update a resource. Unlike PUT, PATCH requests allow for updating only a subset of a resource's attributes.
- **DELETE**: Used to delete existing resources. DELETE requests should remove the specified resource from the server.

By using these HTTP methods appropriately, you provide a clear and standardized way for clients to interact with your API.

Representing Resources as JSON

APIs typically communicate using **JSON (JavaScript Object Notation)**, which is a lightweight and easy-to-read data format. When designing an API, it's crucial to structure your JSON responses consistently.

Example of a Well-Formatted JSON Response

When fetching a list of users, you might return a JSON response like this:

```
{
  "status": "success",
  "data": {
    "users": [
      {
        "id": 1,
        "name": "Alice",
        "email": "alice@example.com"
      },
      {
        "id": 2,
        "name": "Bob",
        "email": "bob@example.com"
      }
    ]
  }
}
```

Key points to keep in mind:

- **Consistent Structure**: Keep the structure of your JSON consistent across all endpoints. For example, always return data inside a "data" object, and use a "status" field to indicate success or failure.
- **Standardized Naming Conventions**: Use a consistent naming convention for fields (like camelCase or snake_case) and stick to it throughout the API.
- **Clear Error Messages**: When returning errors, provide clear and descriptive error messages.

Designing Resource Relationships

Many applications involve relationships between resources. For example, users might have posts, and posts might have comments. When designing your API, you'll need to decide how to represent these relationships in your URIs.

There are two common ways to handle resource relationships:

**Nested Resources**: Represent relationships by nesting URIs. For example:

- **GET** /users/{user_id}/posts: Fetch all posts by a specific user.
- **POST** /users/{user_id}/posts: Create a new post for a specific user.

**Linking Resources**: Keep relationships separate but provide links between related resources in your JSON response. For example:

```
{
  "id": 1,
  "title": "Post Title",
  "content": "This is a post",
  "author": {
    "id": 1,
    "name": "Alice",
    "link": "/users/1"
  }
}
```

Both approaches have their pros and cons. Nested resources provide a clear way to indicate ownership, while linking resources keeps your URIs flatter and may simplify relationships in more complex APIs.

Implementing Pagination and Filtering

When an API returns large collections of resources, it's important to implement pagination to avoid overwhelming the client and server. **Pagination** splits a large collection into smaller, manageable chunks, while **filtering** allows clients to request only the data they need.

Example: Implementing Pagination

A common approach to pagination is to use **query parameters** like page and limit. For example:

- **GET** /users?page=2&limit=20: Fetch the second page of users with 20 users per page.

In your Flask API, you might handle pagination like this:

```
from flask import Flask, request, jsonify

app = Flask(__name__)

users = [{"id": i, "name": f"User {i}"} for i in range(1, 101)]

@app.route('/users', methods=['GET'])
def get_users():
    page = int(request.args.get('page', 1))
    limit = int(request.args.get('limit', 10))
    start = (page - 1) * limit
    end = start + limit
    return jsonify({
        "status": "success",
        "page": page,
        "limit": limit,
        "data": users[start:end]
    })

if __name__ == '__main__':
    app.run(debug=True)
```

This example fetches a specific page of users based on the page and limit query parameters. It calculates the starting and ending indices and returns the appropriate slice of the users list.

Filtering Data

You can also allow clients to filter data based on certain attributes. For example, if your users have an active attribute, you might allow filtering based on whether users are active:

• **GET** /users?active=true: Fetch all active users.

In Flask, you can implement filtering using query parameters:

```
@app.route('/users', methods=['GET'])
def get_users():
    active = request.args.get('active')
    filtered_users = [user for user in users if
    str(user.get('active', False)) == active] if active else users
    return jsonify(filtered_users)
```

By combining pagination and filtering, you provide clients with a flexible and efficient way to interact with your API's resources.

Handling Errors and Status Codes

A well-designed API should return appropriate status codes and clear error messages for different scenarios. This not only improves the client's experience but also makes debugging easier.

Common Status Codes

Here are some common HTTP status codes and when to use them:

- **200 OK**: The request was successful, and the server returned the requested data.
- **201 Created**: A new resource was successfully created.
- **204 No Content**: The request was successful, but there is no data to return.
- **400 Bad Request**: The client sent an invalid request (e.g., missing required parameters).
- **401 Unauthorized**: The client is not authenticated.
- **403 Forbidden**: The client is authenticated but does not have permission to access the resource.
- **404 Not Found**: The requested resource could not be found.
- **500 Internal Server Error**: An unexpected error occurred on the server.

Example: Returning Custom Error Responses

You can create custom error handlers in Flask to return consistent error responses for different scenarios. For example:

```
@app.errorhandler(404)
def not_found(error):
    return jsonify({
        "status": "error",
        "message": "Resource not found"
    }), 404


@app.errorhandler(400)
def bad_request(error):
    return jsonify({
        "status": "error",
        "message": "Bad request"
    }), 400
```

These handlers return a JSON response with a clear error message and the appropriate status code.

Creating Clear and Consistent API Documentation

Good documentation is key to making your API easy to understand and use. It's the interface through which developers will interact with your API, so it needs to be clear, accurate, and up-to-date.

There are several tools available for documenting APIs, including **Swagger** and **Postman**. In this section, we'll briefly discuss how to document your API using Swagger.

Documenting with Swagger

**Swagger** is a popular tool for generating interactive API documentation. It allows developers to see available endpoints, their parameters, and sample responses, and even test the API directly from the documentation page.

You can use the **Flask-Swagger** extension to automatically generate Swagger documentation from your Flask routes. To get started, install the necessary packages:

```
pip install flask-swagger-ui
```

Next, set up Swagger in your Flask app:

```python
from flask import Flask
from flask_swagger_ui import get_swaggerui_blueprint

app = Flask(__name__)

SWAGGER_URL = '/swagger'
API_DOCS = '/static/swagger.json'
swaggerui_blueprint = get_swaggerui_blueprint(SWAGGER_URL,
API_DOCS)

app.register_blueprint(swaggerui_blueprint, url_prefix=SWAGGER_URL)

if __name__ == '__main__':
    app.run(debug=True)
```

This configuration adds a Swagger UI to your application, accessible at /swagger. You can define your API documentation in a swagger.json file in the /static folder. The Swagger UI will read this file and generate an interactive documentation page.

# Working with Databases

D atabases are a fundamental part of almost every web application. They store and manage the data that APIs interact with, enabling the creation, retrieval, updating, and deletion of information. In this chapter, you'll learn how to integrate databases with Flask using SQL and NoSQL solutions, understand Object-Relational Mapping (ORM) with SQLAlchemy, and implement migrations for managing database changes.

Introduction to Databases for Flask APIs

When designing a Flask API, you'll need to decide on a database solution. Flask supports various databases, and the choice between SQL (relational) and NoSQL (non-relational) depends on your project requirements.

**Relational Databases (SQL)**:

- Examples: PostgreSQL, MySQL, SQLite
- Data is organized into tables with predefined schemas.
- Ideal for structured data with complex relationships.

**Non-Relational Databases (NoSQL)**:

- Examples: MongoDB, CouchDB, Redis
- Data is stored as collections of documents, key-value pairs, or graphs.
- Ideal for unstructured or semi-structured data with flexible schemas.

In this chapter, we'll focus on integrating SQL databases using Flask-

SQLAlchemy, which is the most common choice for Flask applications. However, we'll also briefly cover working with NoSQL databases like MongoDB to give you a well-rounded understanding.

Setting Up SQLAlchemy

**SQLAlchemy** is an ORM (Object-Relational Mapping) library that simplifies database interaction by allowing you to work with Python objects instead of writing raw SQL queries. It bridges the gap between Python and relational databases, making it easier to map tables and columns to classes and attributes.

Installing SQLAlchemy and Flask-SQLAlchemy

Before we start, ensure you have Flask-SQLAlchemy installed in your virtual environment. If not, you can install it with the following command:

```
pip install Flask-SQLAlchemy
```

Configuring SQLAlchemy in Flask

Start by setting up a basic Flask application and configuring SQLAlchemy. Create a file named app.py with the following code:

```
from flask import Flask
from flask_sqlalchemy import SQLAlchemy

app = Flask(__name__)

# Configure the SQLAlchemy part of the app instance
app.config['SQLALCHEMY_DATABASE_URI'] = 'sqlite:///site.db'
app.config['SQLALCHEMY_TRACK_MODIFICATIONS'] = False

# Create the SQLAlchemy database instance
db = SQLAlchemy(app)

if __name__ == '__main__':
    app.run(debug=True)
```

**Explanation**:

- SQLALCHEMY_DATABASE_URI specifies the connection string to your database. In this case, we're using SQLite, which stores data in a local file named site.db. You can replace this with a connection string for PostgreSQL, MySQL, or another database if needed.
- SQLALCHEMY_TRACK_MODIFICATIONS disables a feature that tracks modifications to objects and issues signals. It's unnecessary for most cases and incurs overhead, so it's best to disable it.

Creating Database Models

A **model** in SQLAlchemy represents a table in your database, and each model's attributes represent columns. Let's define a basic User model for demonstration:

```python
from app import db

class User(db.Model):
    id = db.Column(db.Integer, primary_key=True)
    username = db.Column(db.String(80), unique=True,
    nullable=False)
    email = db.Column(db.String(120), unique=True, nullable=False)
    password = db.Column(db.String(60), nullable=False)

    def __repr__(self):
        return f"User('{self.username}', '{self.email}')"
```

**Explanation**:

- The User class inherits from db.Model, making it a SQLAlchemy model.
- Each attribute is a column in the users table. We define the column type (Integer, String) and set constraints like primary_key=True for the id column and unique=True or nullable=False where appropriate.

Creating the Database

To create the database and its tables, use the following commands in an interactive Python shell:

```
>>> from app import db
>>> db.create_all()
```

This command creates the database file (site.db) and all tables defined in your models.

Working with Database Records

With your database and model set up, you can now create, read, update, and delete records. Here's how to perform these basic operations:

Adding New Records

To add a new user to the database, follow these steps:

- Open an interactive Python shell and run:

```
>>> from app import db
>>> from app import User
>>> new_user = User(username='Alice', email='alice@example.com',
password='password123')
>>> db.session.add(new_user)
>>> db.session.commit()
```

**Explanation**:

- We created a new instance of the User class.
- The db.session.add() method adds the new user to the session, and db.session.commit() commits the changes to the database.

Querying Records

To fetch users from the database, you can use the following methods:

- **Fetch all users**:

```
>>> users = User.query.all()
>>> print(users)
```

- **Fetch a specific user by username**:

```
>>> user = User.query.filter_by(username='Alice').first()
>>> print(user)
```

- **Fetch a user by their primary key (id)**:

```
>>> user = User.query.get(1)
>>> print(user)
```

Updating Records

To update an existing user's email:

- Fetch the user:

```
>>> user = User.query.get(1)
```

- Update the email:

```
>>> user.email = 'alice_new@example.com'
>>> db.session.commit()
```

Deleting Records

To delete a user:

- Fetch the user:

```
>>> user = User.query.get(1)
```

- Delete the user:

```
>>> db.session.delete(user)
>>> db.session.commit()
```

Using Migrations to Manage Database Changes

As your application evolves, you may need to make changes to your database schema. This is where **migrations** come in. Migrations allow you to modify your database structure without losing existing data.

Installing Flask-Migrate

Flask-Migrate is a popular extension for handling database migrations. To install it, run:

```
pip install Flask-Migrate
```

Configuring Flask-Migrate

Add the following lines to your app.py file:

```
from flask_migrate import Migrate

# Create a migration object
migrate = Migrate(app, db)
```

Creating and Applying Migrations

- **Initialize migrations**: Run this command once to set up migrations for your project:

```
flask db init
```

- **Create a new migration**: Whenever you make changes to your models, create a migration:

```
flask db migrate -m "Added User model"
```

- **Apply the migration**: Run this command to apply the changes to your database:

```
flask db upgrade
```

Working with NoSQL Databases

Flask is not limited to SQL databases. You can also integrate NoSQL databases like **MongoDB**. The **Flask-PyMongo** extension simplifies MongoDB integration.

Installing and Configuring Flask-PyMongo

- Install Flask-PyMongo:

```
pip install Flask-PyMongo
```

- Configure Flask-PyMongo in your app.py:

```
from flask import Flask
from flask_pymongo import PyMongo

app = Flask(__name__)
app.config["MONGO_URI"] = "mongodb://localhost:27017/myDatabase"
mongo = PyMongo(app)
```

## Creating and Querying MongoDB Documents

You can now perform CRUD operations on MongoDB collections:

1. **Insert a new document**:

```
@app.route('/add_user', methods=['POST'])
def add_user():
    user_data = {"name": "Alice", "email": "alice@example.com"}
    mongo.db.users.insert_one(user_data)
    return "User added successfully", 201
```

1. **Query a document**:

```
@app.route('/get_users', methods=['GET'])
def get_users():
    users = mongo.db.users.find()
    return jsonify([user for user in users]), 200
```

Using NoSQL databases like MongoDB can be beneficial for projects that require flexibility in schema design or need to handle large amounts of unstructured data.

## Best Practices for Database Integration

Here are some best practices to keep in mind when integrating databases with Flask:

1. **Use an ORM**: For SQL databases, using an ORM like SQLAlchemy simplifies database interactions and reduces the risk of SQL injection attacks.

2. **Validate Input Data**: Always validate incoming data before inserting or updating records in your database.

3. **Handle Errors Gracefully**: Implement error handling to catch database-related exceptions and return appropriate responses.

4. **Use Migrations**: When working with relational databases, use migrations to manage changes to your database schema.

5. **Optimize Queries**: Minimize the number of queries to the database by using appropriate filters and joins. Use indexes to improve query performance.

# Authentication and Authorization

A uthentication and authorization are critical aspects of API development. They ensure that only authenticated and authorized users can access certain resources or perform specific actions within your application. While authentication verifies the identity of a user, authorization determines whether that user has permission to perform an action.

In this chapter, you will learn how to implement user authentication and manage authorization in your Flask APIs. We will cover several methods for securing your API, including JSON Web Tokens (JWT), OAuth 2.0, and Role-Based Access Control (RBAC).

API Security Basics

Before diving into the implementation, it's essential to understand the difference between authentication and authorization:

- **Authentication**: The process of verifying who a user is. For example, when a user logs in with a username and password, their identity is authenticated.
- **Authorization**: The process of verifying what actions an authenticated user can perform. For example, an admin user might be authorized to delete a resource, while a regular user is not.

Both of these are crucial for securing an API and protecting sensitive data.

Implementing JWT Authentication

**JSON Web Tokens (JWT)** are a popular method for securing APIs. JWTs are compact, self-contained tokens that carry information about the user and can be verified using a digital signature. They are often used for stateless authentication in RESTful APIs.

Installing Flask-JWT-Extended

We will use the **Flask-JWT-Extended** extension to implement JWT authentication in Flask. To get started, install it using:

```
pip install Flask-JWT-Extended
```

Configuring JWT in Flask

Create a basic Flask application and configure JWT as follows:

```
from flask import Flask, jsonify, request
from flask_sqlalchemy import SQLAlchemy
from flask_bcrypt import Bcrypt
from flask_jwt_extended import JWTManager, create_access_token,
jwt_required, get_jwt_identity

app = Flask(__name__)

app.config['SQLALCHEMY_DATABASE_URI'] = 'sqlite:///users.db'
app.config['SQLALCHEMY_TRACK_MODIFICATIONS'] = False
app.config['JWT_SECRET_KEY'] = 'super-secret-key'  # Change this
to a strong secret key

db = SQLAlchemy(app)
bcrypt = Bcrypt(app)
jwt = JWTManager(app)
```

**Explanation**:

- We've configured SQLAlchemy for database interaction, **Bcrypt** for hashing passwords, and **JWTManager** for handling JWTs.
- The JWT_SECRET_KEY is used to sign the JWTs. In a production

environment, you should use a strong, secret key and keep it safe.

## Creating User Models and Registration

Next, create a basic user model and implement a registration endpoint:

```
class User(db.Model):
    id = db.Column(db.Integer, primary_key=True)
    username = db.Column(db.String(80), unique=True,
    nullable=False)
    email = db.Column(db.String(120), unique=True, nullable=False)
    password = db.Column(db.String(60), nullable=False)


@app.route('/register', methods=['POST'])
def register():
    data = request.get_json()
    hashed_password =
    bcrypt.generate_password_hash(data['password']).decode('utf-8')
    new_user = User(username=data['username'],
    email=data['email'], password=hashed_password)
    db.session.add(new_user)
    db.session.commit()
    return jsonify({"message": "User registered successfully"}),
    201
```

## Implementing Login and Token Generation

Now, implement a login route that verifies the user's credentials and returns a JWT:

```
@app.route('/login', methods=['POST'])
def login():
    data = request.get_json()
    user = User.query.filter_by(username=data['username']).first()

    if user and bcrypt.check_password_hash(user.password,
    data['password']):
        access_token = create_access_token(identity={'username':
        user.username, 'email': user.email})
        return jsonify({"access_token": access_token}), 200
```

```
return jsonify({"message": "Invalid credentials"}), 401
```

**Explanation**:

- The login route checks if the username exists and if the password matches the hashed password stored in the database.
- If the credentials are correct, it generates an access token using create_ac cess_token() and returns it to the client.

Protecting Routes with JWT

You can now protect routes using the @jwt_required() decorator. This decorator ensures that only authenticated users can access the route.

```
@app.route('/protected', methods=['GET'])
@jwt_required()
def protected():
    current_user = get_jwt_identity()
    return jsonify({"message": f"Hello,
    {current_user['username']}!"}), 200
```

**Explanation**:

- The @jwt_required() decorator requires a valid JWT to access this route.
- The get_jwt_identity() function retrieves the identity of the currently logged-in user from the JWT.

Implementing Role-Based Access Control (RBAC)

Once you have basic authentication in place, you may want to implement role-based access control (RBAC) to restrict certain actions to specific roles (e.g., admin, user). This can be achieved by adding a role attribute to your user model and checking the user's role in protected routes.

Updating the User Model with Roles

Modify your User model to include a role:

```
class User(db.Model):
    id = db.Column(db.Integer, primary_key=True)
    username = db.Column(db.String(80), unique=True,
    nullable=False)
    email = db.Column(db.String(120), unique=True, nullable=False)
    password = db.Column(db.String(60), nullable=False)
    role = db.Column(db.String(20), nullable=False, default='user')
```

## Creating an Admin-Only Route

You can then create a route that only admin users can access:

```
@app.route('/admin', methods=['GET'])
@jwt_required()
def admin():
    current_user = get_jwt_identity()

    if current_user['role'] != 'admin':
        return jsonify({"message": "Access forbidden: Admins
        only"}), 403

    return jsonify({"message": "Welcome, admin!"}), 200
```

**Explanation**:

- The @jwt_required() decorator ensures that the user is authenticated.
- We check the user's role and return a **403 Forbidden** response if the user is not an admin.

## Implementing OAuth 2.0 Authentication

OAuth 2.0 is another popular authentication method used for granting third-party access to your APIs without sharing user credentials. With OAuth 2.0, you can allow users to log in to your application using external providers like Google, Facebook, or GitHub.

Using Flask-Dance for OAuth 2.0

**Flask-Dance** is a popular extension for implementing OAuth 2.0 in Flask.

It provides pre-built integrations with various OAuth providers.
First, install Flask-Dance:

```
pip install Flask-Dance
```

## Setting Up Google OAuth

1. **Register Your Application**: Go to the **Google Developer Console** and register your application to obtain a **Client ID** and **Client Secret**.
2. **Configure Flask-Dance**:

```
from flask_dance.contrib.google import make_google_blueprint,
google

google_bp = make_google_blueprint(client_id="your-client-id",
client_secret="your-client-secret", redirect_to="google_login")

app.register_blueprint(google_bp, url_prefix="/login")

@app.route('/google_login')
def google_login():
    if not google.authorized:
        return redirect(url_for("google.login"))

    resp = google.get("/plus/v1/people/me")
    assert resp.ok, resp.text

    return jsonify(resp.json())
```

**Explanation**:

- The make_google_blueprint() function sets up a blueprint for Google OAuth.
- The /google_login route checks if the user is authorized. If not, it redirects the user to Google's login page.

- Upon successful login, it retrieves user information from Google and displays it as JSON.

This setup allows users to log in using their Google accounts without having to create a separate username and password for your application.

Best Practices for API Security

Securing your API is an ongoing process. Here are some best practices to keep in mind:

1. **Use HTTPS**: Always use HTTPS to encrypt data in transit between the client and server. This prevents attackers from intercepting sensitive information.
2. **Validate Input Data**: Validate all incoming data to protect against SQL injection, XSS, and other common attacks.
3. **Limit Token Lifetimes**: Keep the lifetimes of JWTs short and refresh tokens periodically to minimize security risks.
4. **Use Secure Password Hashing**: Use a strong password hashing algorithm like **Bcrypt** or **Argon2** to store user passwords securely.
5. **Rate Limiting**: Implement rate limiting to protect your API from brute-force attacks and denial-of-service attacks.
6. **Implement Proper Logging and Monitoring**: Keep detailed logs of authentication attempts and monitor them for suspicious activity.

# Error Handling and Validation

A robust API must be able to handle errors gracefully and validate incoming data effectively. Proper error handling ensures that your API provides clear and consistent messages to clients when something goes wrong. Meanwhile, input validation helps maintain the integrity of your application by preventing invalid or malicious data from being processed.

In this chapter, you will learn how to implement error handling and data validation in Flask. We will cover strategies for handling common errors, returning appropriate HTTP status codes, and validating incoming requests using various tools and techniques.

Handling Errors in Flask APIs

Errors can occur for many reasons, such as invalid input, missing resources, or unauthorized access. It's important to handle these errors gracefully and return meaningful responses to the client.

**Flask** provides built-in mechanisms for handling errors using decorators and custom error handlers. Let's explore these concepts with examples.

Custom Error Handlers

Custom error handlers allow you to define how your API responds to specific types of errors. For instance, you might want to return a 404 error when a requested resource is not found or a 400 error for invalid input.

Here's how to create a custom error handler in Flask:

```python
from flask import Flask, jsonify

app = Flask(__name__)

@app.errorhandler(404)
def not_found(error):
    return jsonify({
        "status": "error",
        "message": "Resource not found"
    }), 404

@app.errorhandler(400)
def bad_request(error):
    return jsonify({
        "status": "error",
        "message": "Bad request"
    }), 400
```

## Explanation:

- The @app.errorhandler decorator is used to register custom error handlers for specific HTTP status codes.
- When a 404 or 400 error occurs, Flask will automatically call the corresponding function and return the JSON response.

Handling 500 Internal Server Errors

A **500 Internal Server Error** occurs when there is an unexpected issue on the server side. You can create a custom handler for 500 errors to provide a more user-friendly response:

```python
@app.errorhandler(500)
def internal_server_error(error):
    return jsonify({
        "status": "error",
        "message": "An internal error occurred. Please try again
        later."
```

```
    }), 500
```

It's also a good practice to log these errors for debugging purposes. You can use Python's built-in logging module to log detailed error information:

```
import logging

logging.basicConfig(filename='app.log', level=logging.ERROR)

@app.errorhandler(500)
def internal_server_error(error):
    logging.error(f"Server Error: {error}")
    return jsonify({
        "status": "error",
        "message": "An internal error occurred. Please try again
        later."
    }), 500
```

## Returning Proper HTTP Status Codes

An essential part of error handling is returning appropriate HTTP status codes. These codes help clients understand the outcome of their requests. Below are some common status codes and when to use them:

- **200 OK**: The request was successful, and the server returned the requested data.
- **201 Created**: A new resource was successfully created.
- **204 No Content**: The request was successful, but there is no data to return.
- **400 Bad Request**: The client sent an invalid request, such as missing required fields or incorrect data types.
- **401 Unauthorized**: The client is not authenticated.
- **403 Forbidden**: The client is authenticated but does not have permission to access the resource.
- **404 Not Found**: The requested resource could not be found.
- **500 Internal Server Error**: An unexpected error occurred on the server.

Using the correct status codes helps clients interpret your API's responses accurately.

Validating Input with Marshmallow

**Marshmallow** is a popular library for object serialization and input validation in Python. It works seamlessly with Flask and allows you to define schemas for validating and deserializing incoming data.

Installing Marshmallow

To get started with Marshmallow, install it using:

```
pip install marshmallow
```

Creating a Marshmallow Schema

Define a Marshmallow schema to specify the expected structure of incoming data. Let's create a schema for user registration:

```
from marshmallow import Schema, fields, validate, ValidationError

class UserSchema(Schema):
    username = fields.String(required=True,
        validate=validate.Length(min=3, max=20))
    email = fields.Email(required=True)
    password = fields.String(required=True,
        validate=validate.Length(min=6))
```

**Explanation**:

- The UserSchema class inherits from Schema and defines fields with specific validation rules.
- We've used the validate.Length() method to enforce length constraints on the username and password fields.
- The fields.Email validator automatically checks if the email field contains a valid email address.

Validating Input Data

You can now use the schema to validate incoming data in your route:

```
from flask import request

@app.route('/register', methods=['POST'])
def register():
    user_schema = UserSchema()
    try:
        data = user_schema.load(request.get_json())
    except ValidationError as err:
        return jsonify({"errors": err.messages}), 400

    # If validation passes, proceed with user registration
    # Create a new user and save to the database
    return jsonify({"message": "User registered successfully"}),
    201
```

**Explanation**:

- The user_schema.load() method validates the incoming data and deserializes it into a Python dictionary.
- If the data is invalid, Marshmallow raises a ValidationError, and we return a 400 response with the error messages.

Custom Validation with Marshmallow

You can define custom validation functions for more complex validation scenarios. For example, you might want to check if a username contains only alphanumeric characters:

```
def validate_username(username):
    if not username.isalnum():
        raise ValidationError("Username must contain only letters
        and numbers")

class UserSchema(Schema):
```

```
username = fields.String(required=True,
validate=validate.And(validate.Length(min=3, max=20),
validate_username))
email = fields.Email(required=True)
password = fields.String(required=True,
validate=validate.Length(min=6))
```

## Explanation:

- We defined a custom function validate_username that raises a Validation-Error if the username contains non-alphanumeric characters.
- We added the custom validator to the username field using validate.And().

Returning Consistent Error Responses

Consistent error responses make it easier for clients to understand and handle errors. For instance, you might want to standardize your error responses to include fields like status, message, and details (if applicable).

Here's an example of a consistent error response:

```
@app.errorhandler(404)
def not_found(error):
    return jsonify({
        "status": "error",
        "message": "Resource not found",
        "details": str(error)
    }), 404
```

By using a consistent format for all error responses, you can improve the overall experience for API consumers.

Input Validation in Flask Using Flask-WTF

Another option for input validation in Flask is **Flask-WTF**, which integrates **WTForms** with Flask. WTForms is a powerful form-handling library that supports input validation and CSRF protection.

Installing Flask-WTF

To get started with Flask-WTF, install it using:

```
pip install Flask-WTF
```

## Creating a Flask-WTF Form

Define a form class using WTForms to specify the expected fields and their validation rules:

```
from flask_wtf import FlaskForm
from wtforms import StringField, PasswordField
from wtforms.validators import DataRequired, Email, Length

class RegistrationForm(FlaskForm):
    username = StringField('Username', validators=[DataRequired(),
    Length(min=3, max=20)])
    email = StringField('Email', validators=[DataRequired(),
    Email()])
    password = PasswordField('Password',
    validators=[DataRequired(), Length(min=6)])
```

## Validating Form Data in a Route

You can use the form class to validate incoming data in a route:

```
from flask import Flask, request, jsonify

app = Flask(__name__)
app.config['SECRET_KEY'] = 'secret'

@app.route('/register', methods=['POST'])
def register():
    form = RegistrationForm()

    if not form.validate_on_submit():
        return jsonify({"errors": form.errors}), 400

    # If validation passes, proceed with user registration
    # Create a new user and save to the database
```

```
return jsonify({"message": "User registered successfully"}),
201
```

**Explanation**:

- The form.validate_on_submit() method checks if the incoming request contains valid form data.
- If validation fails, we return a 400 response with the error messages.

Logging and Debugging Errors

Effective error handling also involves logging errors and providing sufficient debugging information during development. Flask's built-in logging capabilities allow you to log error messages, which can be invaluable for diagnosing issues.

Logging Errors in Flask

You can use Python's built-in logging module to log errors:

```
import logging

logging.basicConfig(filename='app.log', level=logging.ERROR)

@app.errorhandler(500)
def internal_server_error(error):
    logging.error(f"Server Error: {error}")
    return jsonify({
        "status": "error",
        "message": "An internal error occurred. Please try again
        later."
    }), 500
```

**Explanation**:

- The logging.error() function logs detailed error information to a file named app.log.
- This approach is especially useful in production environments where

detailed error messages should not be exposed to clients.

Enabling Flask's Debug Mode

During development, you can enable Flask's debug mode to get detailed error information in the browser:

```
if __name__ == '__main__':
    app.run(debug=True)
```

With debug mode enabled, Flask will provide a stack trace whenever an error occurs, making it easier to identify the source of the problem.

# Versioning and Documentation

As your API evolves, you'll need to make changes that might break existing functionality. This is where **API versioning** comes in. Versioning ensures that changes in your API do not disrupt existing clients by allowing different versions of the API to coexist. At the same time, **documentation** is crucial for providing developers with clear guidance on how to use your API.

In this chapter, you'll learn various strategies for versioning your API and how to document it using tools like Swagger and Postman. These practices will help maintain backward compatibility, provide clear migration paths, and make your API easy to understand and consume.

Strategies for API Versioning

API versioning is the practice of managing changes to your API in a way that doesn't disrupt existing clients. There are several ways to version an API, each with its own advantages and trade-offs.

**URI Versioning (Path Versioning)**: This is one of the most common versioning strategies, where the version number is included in the URI.

**Example**:

/api/v1/users

/api/v2/users

- **Pros**:
- Simple to understand and implement.
- Explicit versioning in the URL makes it clear which version is being

accessed.

- **Cons**:
- Can result in duplicated logic and code across versions.
- May lead to bloated URLs as the number of versions grows.

**Header Versioning**: Version information is provided in the HTTP request headers.

**Example**:

```
GET /users HTTP/1.1
Accept: application/vnd.yourapp.v1+json
```

- **Pros**:
- Keeps the URI clean and avoids redundancy.
- Can handle multiple versions more gracefully.
- **Cons**:
- Clients must be aware of the required headers.
- Slightly more complex to implement and maintain.

**Query Parameter Versioning**: The version is specified as a query parameter in the URI.

**Example**:

/api/users?version=1

- **Pros**:
- Easy to add versioning to existing endpoints.
- Provides flexibility to specify versions dynamically.
- **Cons**:
- Not as clean or explicit as path-based versioning.
- Potential for inconsistent usage of query parameters.

**Content Negotiation Versioning**: Uses the **Accept** header to specify the

API version. This strategy is similar to header versioning but focuses on content types.

**Example**:

```
GET /users HTTP/1.1
Accept: application/vnd.yourapp+json; version=1.0
```

- **Pros**:
- Keeps the URI clean.
- Allows for flexible versioning based on content types.
- **Cons**:
- Requires additional implementation effort on the server side.
- Clients need to be aware of the Accept header's format.

Implementing Versioning in Flask

We'll implement a simple example of **URI versioning** in Flask to illustrate the concept. Consider the following scenario where you have an API with two versions:

1. **Version 1**: Returns a list of users with basic information.
2. **Version 2**: Returns a list of users with additional fields like email and role.

Step 1: Define Versioned Routes

In your app.py file, define separate routes for each version:

```
from flask import Flask, jsonify

app = Flask(__name__)

# Data for demonstration purposes
users_v1 = [
```

```
      {"id": 1, "name": "Alice"},
      {"id": 2, "name": "Bob"}
  ]

users_v2 = [
      {"id": 1, "name": "Alice", "email": "alice@example.com",
      "role": "admin"},
      {"id": 2, "name": "Bob", "email": "bob@example.com", "role":
      "user"}
  ]

# Version 1 route
@app.route('/api/v1/users', methods=['GET'])
def get_users_v1():
      return jsonify(users_v1)

# Version 2 route
@app.route('/api/v2/users', methods=['GET'])
def get_users_v2():
      return jsonify(users_v2)

if __name__ == '__main__':
      app.run(debug=True)
```

In this example:

- The /api/v1/users route returns basic user information.
- The /api/v2/users route returns more detailed user information, including email and role.

Clients can choose which version of the API to use by specifying the
appropriate URI.

Maintaining Backward Compatibility

One of the primary goals of API versioning is to maintain backward
compatibility. When making changes to your API, consider the following
best practices:

1. **Deprecate Gradually**: Notify clients in advance when a version is being deprecated and provide a clear timeline for when it will be phased out.
2. **Provide Clear Migration Paths**: Document differences between versions and provide clear instructions on how to migrate to the latest version.
3. **Avoid Breaking Changes**: Whenever possible, introduce non-breaking changes or additions in new versions to minimize disruption for existing clients.

Documenting APIs with Swagger

**Swagger** (now part of the **OpenAPI** specification) is a popular tool for generating interactive API documentation. It allows developers to explore and test API endpoints directly from a web-based interface.

Setting Up Swagger with Flask-RESTful

To integrate Swagger with Flask, we'll use the **Flask-RESTful** and **Flask-Swagger-UI** extensions.

- **Install Flask-RESTful and Flask-Swagger-UI**:

```
pip install flask-restful flask-swagger-ui
```

- **Create a Simple API with Flask-RESTful**:

```
from flask import Flask
from flask_restful import Resource, Api

app = Flask(__name__)
api = Api(app)

class UserList(Resource):
```

```
    def get(self):
        return {"users": [{"id": 1, "name": "Alice"}, {"id": 2,
        "name": "Bob"}]}

api.add_resource(UserList, '/api/v1/users')

if __name__ == '__main__':
    app.run(debug=True)
```

- **Setting Up Swagger UI**:

Create a swagger.json file in your project's root directory with the following content:

```
{
  "swagger": "2.0",
  "info": {
    "title": "User API",
    "description": "API for managing users",
    "version": "1.0.0"
  },
  "paths": {
    "/api/v1/users": {
      "get": {
        "summary": "Get a list of users",
        "responses": {
          "200": {
            "description": "A JSON array of user names",
            "schema": {
              "type": "array",
              "items": {
                "type": "object",
                "properties": {
                  "id": {
                    "type": "integer"
                  },
                  "name": {
```

```
                    "type": "string"
                  }
                }
              }
            }
          }
        }
      }
    }
  }
}
```

- **Add Swagger UI to Your Flask App**:

```python
from flask import Flask
from flask_swagger_ui import get_swaggerui_blueprint

app = Flask(__name__)

SWAGGER_URL = '/swagger'
API_DOCS_URL = '/swagger.json'

swaggerui_blueprint = get_swaggerui_blueprint(SWAGGER_URL,
API_DOCS_URL)

app.register_blueprint(swaggerui_blueprint, url_prefix=SWAGGER_URL)

if __name__ == '__main__':
    app.run(debug=True)
```

Now, when you visit /swagger, you'll see an interactive documentation page where you can test your API endpoints.

Documenting APIs with Postman

**Postman** is another popular tool for documenting and testing APIs. It allows you to create collections of requests, add descriptions, and share them with others.

Creating a Postman Collection

1. **Create a New Collection**: In Postman, create a new collection and name it something like "**User API v1**".
2. **Add Requests to the Collection**: Create requests for each API endpoint (e.g., GET /api/v1/users), and add them to your collection.
3. **Add Descriptions**: For each request, add descriptions and expected responses to provide context for developers using your API.
4. **Export and Share the Collection**: You can export the collection as a **JSON** file and share it with other developers. Alternatively, you can publish the collection using Postman's **documentation feature**.

Best Practices for API Documentation

Good documentation helps developers understand and use your API effectively. Here are some best practices for creating API documentation:

1. **Provide Clear Descriptions**: Each endpoint should have a clear description of its purpose and how to use it.
2. **Specify Input and Output Formats**: Clearly define the required input parameters, headers, and expected JSON structures for both requests and responses.
3. **Use Examples**: Provide example requests and responses to illustrate the expected behavior.
4. **Keep Documentation Up-to-Date**: As your API evolves, make sure your documentation reflects any changes or new features.

# Testing and Debugging APIs

T horough testing and effective debugging are essential to ensure that your API functions as expected and is reliable in production. Testing helps identify bugs, verify functionality, and validate that your API meets requirements, while debugging enables you to track down and resolve issues efficiently.

In this chapter, we'll explore different types of testing, including unit testing and integration testing. You'll learn how to use tools like **Pytest, Flask-Testing**, and **Postman** to test your API. We'll also cover common debugging techniques and logging practices to streamline the development process.

Types of Tests for APIs

When testing APIs, there are several types of tests you should consider:

1. **Unit Tests**: Focus on testing individual functions or components in isolation. For example, you might write a unit test to verify that a specific function correctly validates input data.
2. **Integration Tests**: Verify that different components of the application work together as expected. For example, you might test a route to ensure that it interacts correctly with the database.
3. **Functional Tests**: Test the behavior of the API from the client's perspective, simulating real-world scenarios.
4. **End-to-End (E2E) Tests**: Cover the entire workflow, from sending an HTTP request to receiving and validating the response.

Unit Testing Flask APIs with Pytest

**Pytest** is a popular testing framework for Python that makes it easy to write and run tests. Let's start by writing some basic unit tests for your Flask API.

Installing Pytest

To get started, install Pytest in your project's virtual environment:

```
pip install pytest
```

Setting Up a Test File

Create a file named test_app.py in your project's root directory. In this file, you'll define your test functions.

**Setting Up a Test Client**:

Create a fixture to set up a test client using Pytest:

```
import pytest
from app import app

@pytest.fixture
def client():
    with app.test_client() as client:
        yield client
```

**Explanation**:

- The app.test_client() function creates a test client that simulates requests to your Flask app. You can use this client to send HTTP requests to your API endpoints during testing.

**Writing Basic Unit Tests**:

Here's an example of a basic unit test for a GET request to your /users route:

```
def test_get_users(client):
    response = client.get('/api/v1/users')
    assert response.status_code == 200
    assert response.is_json
    assert len(response.get_json()["users"]) > 0
```

## Explanation:

- The test sends a GET request to /api/v1/users using the test client.
- It asserts that the response status code is 200 and that the response is in JSON format.
- It checks that the list of users returned is not empty.

## Running the Tests:

To run your tests, execute the following command in your terminal:

```
pytest
```

1. Pytest will discover and run all test functions that start with the prefix test_.

Integration Testing with Flask-Testing

**Flask-Testing** is an extension for writing integration tests in Flask. It provides additional features, such as testing database interactions and handling teardown operations.

Installing Flask-Testing

To get started with Flask-Testing, install it using:

```
pip install Flask-Testing
```

Setting Up Integration Tests

Here's an example of how to write integration tests using Flask-Testing:

**Creating a Test Class**:

Create a test class that inherits from TestCase:

```python
from flask_testing import TestCase
from app import app, db, User


class UserTestCase(TestCase):

    def create_app(self):
        app.config['TESTING'] = True
        app.config['SQLALCHEMY_DATABASE_URI'] =
        'sqlite:///:memory:'
        return app

    def setUp(self):
        db.create_all()
        user = User(username="TestUser", email="test@example.com",
        password="password123")
        db.session.add(user)
        db.session.commit()

    def tearDown(self):
        db.session.remove()
        db.drop_all()
```

**Explanation**:

- The create_app() method configures the Flask app for testing.
- The setUp() method sets up a fresh database for each test and adds a test user.
- The tearDown() method cleans up the database after each test.

**Writing Integration Tests**:

You can now write tests that interact with the database and verify that your routes work as expected:

```python
def test_get_users(self):
    response = self.client.get('/api/v1/users')
    self.assertEqual(response.status_code, 200)
    self.assertTrue(response.is_json)
    data = response.get_json()
    self.assertEqual(len(data['users']), 1)
```

**Explanation**:

- The test sends a GET request to /api/v1/users using the test client.
- It verifies that the response status code is 200 and that the response is in JSON format.
- It checks that the list of users contains exactly one user (the one created in the setUp() method).

Functional Testing with Postman

While unit and integration tests are automated and run within your development environment, **functional tests** can be performed using tools like **Postman**. Postman allows you to simulate real-world scenarios and verify the behavior of your API endpoints.

Creating Postman Tests

- **Set Up a Collection**: Create a collection in Postman for your API and add requests for each endpoint you want to test.
- **Add Test Scripts**: For each request, you can write test scripts using JavaScript. Here's an example script for a GET request to /api/v1/users:

```javascript
pm.test("Status code is 200", function () {
    pm.response.to.have.status(200);
});

pm.test("Response is JSON", function () {
    pm.response.to.be.json;
```

```
});

pm.test("Users list is not empty", function () {
    var jsonData = pm.response.json();
    pm.expect(jsonData.users.length).to.be.above(0);
});
```

- **Run the Tests**: You can run your tests manually in Postman or automate them using **Postman's Collection Runner**. This feature allows you to run all tests in a collection and view detailed results.

Mocking API Responses with the Responses Library

In some cases, you may want to **mock** external API responses to test your application's behavior without relying on actual external services. The **responses** library allows you to mock HTTP responses in your tests.

Installing the Responses Library

Install the responses library using:

```
pip install responses
```

Mocking External API Calls

Here's an example of how to use the responses library to mock an external API call:

```
import responses

@responses.activate
def test_external_api_call(client):
    # Mock the external API response
    responses.add(responses.GET, 'https://api.example.com/data',
                  json={"key": "value"}, status=200)

    # Make a request to the route that calls the external API
    response = client.get('/api/v1/external-data')
```

```
assert response.status_code == 200
assert response.get_json() == {"key": "value"}
```

**Explanation**:

- The @responses.activate decorator enables the mocking of HTTP responses.
- The responses.add() function defines a mock response for a specific URL and HTTP method.
- The test sends a request to your route and verifies that the mocked response is returned.

Automating Tests with CI/CD

As your project grows, automating your tests becomes crucial. By integrating automated tests into your **CI/CD pipeline**, you can catch issues early and ensure that your API remains reliable.

**Setting Up GitHub Actions**: You can use **GitHub Actions** to run your tests automatically whenever you push changes to your repository. Here's an example configuration for a .github/workflows/test.yml file:

```
name: Run Tests

on: [push, pull_request]

jobs:
  build:
    runs-on: ubuntu-latest

    steps:
    - uses: actions/checkout@v2
    - name: Set up Python
      uses: actions/setup-python@v2
      with:
        python-version: '3.x'
    - name: Install dependencies
```

```
  run: |
    python -m pip install --upgrade pip
    pip install -r requirements.txt
- name: Run tests
  run: |
    pytest
```

**Explanation**:

- The workflow runs on each push or pull request.
- It checks out your code, sets up Python, installs dependencies, and runs the tests using pytest.

Debugging API Issues

When debugging your API, it's important to have clear visibility into what's happening in your application. Here are some debugging techniques to help you identify and fix issues:

**Use Flask's Debug Mode**: During development, enable Flask's debug mode to get detailed error messages and stack traces in your browser:

```
if __name__ == '__main__':
    app.run(debug=True)
```

**Log Error Messages**: Use Python's built-in logging module to log error messages and other critical information:

```
import logging

logging.basicConfig(filename='app.log', level=logging.DEBUG)
logging.debug("Debug message")
logging.info("Informational message")
logging.warning("Warning message")
logging.error("Error message")
```

```
logging.critical("Critical message")
```

**Use Breakpoints and Debuggers**: You can use the built-in Python **PDB debugger** or an IDE like PyCharm or VS Code to set breakpoints and step through your code.

```
import pdb; pdb.set_trace()
```

**Monitor API Logs**: In production, monitor your API logs for error messages, performance issues, and suspicious activity. Use centralized logging solutions like **ELK Stack**, **Graylog**, or **Splunk** to aggregate and analyze logs.

# Asynchronous API Development

As APIs scale in size and complexity, the need for efficient handling of concurrent requests becomes more critical. **Asynchronous programming** allows APIs to handle multiple requests simultaneously, improving performance and scalability. By adopting an asynchronous approach, you can optimize your Flask API to manage I/O-bound operations like database access, API calls, and file handling more efficiently.

In this chapter, you'll explore the fundamentals of asynchronous programming, how to implement asynchronous routes in Flask using tools like **AsyncIO** and **Quart**, and best practices for handling asynchronous tasks and database interactions.

Why Go Asynchronous?

Traditional web applications operate synchronously, where each request is handled one at a time. While this approach is simple to understand and implement, it can lead to bottlenecks in I/O-heavy applications. For example:

- When a route performs a database query or makes an external API call, it waits for the response before moving on. This waiting period consumes valuable server resources and limits the number of concurrent requests that the application can handle.
- File processing tasks, such as reading or writing large files, can block the application and affect its overall performance.

By switching to an **asynchronous** approach, you allow your server to process other requests while waiting for I/O-bound tasks to complete.

Asynchronous Programming with AsyncIO

**AsyncIO** is the standard library for asynchronous programming in Python. It provides an event loop that enables concurrent execution of coroutines (special functions defined with async def and called with await). Let's start by understanding the basics of AsyncIO and how it can be applied in API development.

Basics of AsyncIO

- **Coroutines**: Functions defined using async def. They represent tasks that can be paused and resumed, allowing other tasks to run concurrently.

```python
import asyncio

async def greet():
    print("Hello")
    await asyncio.sleep(1)
    print("World")
```

In this example, greet is a coroutine that waits for one second between printing "Hello" and "World".

- **Event Loop**: The event loop is responsible for scheduling and executing coroutines. You can create an event loop and run coroutines as follows:

```python
asyncio.run(greet())
```

- **Awaiting Coroutines**: You can use await to pause the execution of a coroutine until another coroutine finishes.

```
async def main():
    await greet()

asyncio.run(main())
```

By utilizing these concepts, you can build asynchronous APIs that efficiently handle multiple I/O-bound tasks simultaneously.

Asynchronous APIs with Quart

While Flask is a powerful and widely used framework, it does not natively support asynchronous programming. Instead, you can use **Quart**, a Flask-like asynchronous framework built on top of AsyncIO. Quart offers full compatibility with Flask but adds support for asynchronous routes and middleware.

Installing Quart

To get started with Quart, install it using:

```
pip install quart
```

Creating a Simple Asynchronous API with Quart

Let's create a simple API using Quart to demonstrate how asynchronous routes work.

**Setting Up a Basic Quart App**:

```
from quart import Quart, jsonify
import asyncio

app = Quart(__name__)

@app.route('/async_greet', methods=['GET'])
async def async_greet():
```

```
    await asyncio.sleep(1)
    return jsonify({"message": "Hello, Async World!"})

if __name__ == '__main__':
    app.run(debug=True)
```

## Explanation:

- The route async_greet is defined as an asynchronous function using async def.
- The function uses await to pause for one second, simulating an I/O-bound operation.
- The route returns a JSON response with a greeting message.

## Running the Quart App:

To run the app, use the following command:

```
python app.py
```

## Testing the Asynchronous Route:

You can test the route by visiting http://127.0.0.1:5000/async_greet in your browser or using a tool like Postman. You'll notice a one-second delay before receiving the response, which demonstrates the asynchronous behavior.

Asynchronous Database Access with AsyncSQLAlchemy

To achieve full asynchronicity in your API, you also need to implement asynchronous database access. This can be done using **AsyncSQLAlchemy** or **Gino**, which provide asynchronous database integration.

Using SQLAlchemy with AsyncIO

## Installing SQLAlchemy Asyncio Extension:

```
pip install sqlalchemy asyncpg
```

## Setting Up Asynchronous Database Models:

```python
from sqlalchemy.ext.asyncio import create_async_engine,
AsyncSession
from sqlalchemy.orm import sessionmaker, declarative_base
from sqlalchemy import Column, Integer, String

Base = declarative_base()

class User(Base):
    __tablename__ = 'users'
    id = Column(Integer, primary_key=True)
    username = Column(String(50), unique=True)
    email = Column(String(100))

# Configure the asynchronous engine and session
engine =
create_async_engine('postgresql+asyncpg://user:password@localhost/mydb')
AsyncSessionLocal = sessionmaker(bind=engine, class_=AsyncSession,
expire_on_commit=False)
```

## Performing Asynchronous Database Operations:

```python
from quart import Quart, jsonify
from sqlalchemy.ext.asyncio import AsyncSession
from sqlalchemy.future import select

app = Quart(__name__)

@app.route('/users', methods=['GET'])
async def get_users():
    async with AsyncSessionLocal() as session:
        result = await session.execute(select(User))
        users = result.scalars().all()
        return jsonify([{"id": user.id, "username": user.username,
        "email": user.email} for user in users])

if __name__ == '__main__':
    app.run(debug=True)
```

**Explanation**:

- The database engine and session are configured for asynchronous access using create_async_engine and AsyncSession.
- The route get_users uses await to asynchronously query the database for users.

Handling Background Tasks with Celery

Asynchronous programming is great for handling I/O-bound tasks, but for **long-running background tasks** (such as sending emails, processing large files, or generating reports), you might want to use a task queue like **Celery**.

Installing Celery

To get started with Celery, install it using:

```
pip install celery
```

You'll also need a message broker like **Redis** or **RabbitMQ**. For simplicity, we'll use Redis in this example.

Setting Up Celery with Quart

**Configure Celery**:

```
from celery import Celery

def make_celery(app):
    celery = Celery(
        app.import_name,
        backend=app.config['CELERY_RESULT_BACKEND'],
        broker=app.config['CELERY_BROKER_URL']
    )
    celery.conf.update(app.config)
    return celery

app = Quart(__name__)
app.config.update(
```

```
    CELERY_BROKER_URL='redis://localhost:6379/0',
    CELERY_RESULT_BACKEND='redis://localhost:6379/0'
)

celery = make_celery(app)
```

## Defining a Celery Task:

```
@celery.task
def send_email_task(email, message):
    # Simulate sending an email
    print(f"Sending email to {email}: {message}")
```

## Triggering the Task from a Route:

```
@app.route('/send_email', methods=['POST'])
async def send_email():
    data = await request.get_json()
    send_email_task.delay(data['email'], data['message'])
    return jsonify({"message": "Email task started"}), 202
```

## Explanation:

- The send_email_task function simulates sending an email. It is decorated with @celery.task to register it as a background task.
- The route /send_email triggers the task asynchronously using send_email_task.delay().

Best Practices for Asynchronous APIs

Asynchronous programming can improve the performance and scalability of your APIs, but it also introduces complexity. Here are some best practices to follow:

1. **Use Asynchronous Libraries**: Ensure that all libraries and frameworks you use are asynchronous. Mixing synchronous and asynchronous code

can lead to blocking and degrade performance.

2. **Handle Exceptions Gracefully**: Asynchronous tasks can fail, so it's essential to handle exceptions gracefully and provide clear error messages to clients.

3. **Monitor Performance**: Use performance monitoring tools to track the behavior of your asynchronous routes and identify bottlenecks.

4. **Optimize Task Queues**: For long-running tasks, use a task queue like Celery to offload work to background workers. Configure Celery workers to match the expected workload.

# API Optimization and Performance

Optimizing API performance is crucial for creating a fast, responsive, and scalable application, especially as traffic grows. Efficient APIs help reduce latency, minimize server load, and enhance user experience. In this chapter, you'll explore various techniques and best practices for optimizing your Flask API, focusing on reducing response times, handling high traffic loads, and improving the overall efficiency of your application.

1. Profiling and Monitoring Your API

Before optimizing your API, it's essential to understand where bottlenecks are occurring. **Profiling** and **monitoring** allow you to identify these performance issues and decide on effective optimization strategies.

Profiling Tools

- **Flask Profiler**: A simple tool for profiling Flask applications. It helps identify which routes are taking the most time to execute.
- **Installation**: pip install flask-profiler
- **Usage**:

```
from flask import Flask
import flask_profiler

app = Flask(__name__)
```

```
app.config["flask_profiler"] = {
    "enabled": True,
    "storage": {
        "engine": "sqlite"
    },
    "basicAuth": {
        "enabled": False
    }
}

flask_profiler.init_app(app)
```

- **cProfile**: A built-in Python tool that provides detailed profiling of your entire application. It gives insights into where your code spends the most time.
- **Usage**: Run your Flask application with cProfile:

```
python -m cProfile -o output.pstats app.py
```

- You can analyze the generated output using tools like **SnakeViz**.

Monitoring Tools

- **Prometheus and Grafana**: These tools are popular for monitoring and visualizing metrics in real time. They allow you to track metrics like request count, response time, error rate, and memory usage.
- **New Relic** or **Datadog**: These are application performance monitoring tools that can provide deep insights into your API's behavior in production.

2. Caching Responses

**Caching** is an effective way to reduce latency and server load by storing copies of responses and reusing them for identical requests. Flask can be integrated with caching tools like **Redis** or **Flask-Caching** to reduce redundant computation and database queries.

Using Flask-Caching

## Installation:

```
pip install Flask-Caching
```

## Setup:

```python
from flask import Flask
from flask_caching import Cache

app = Flask(__name__)
cache = Cache(app, config={'CACHE_TYPE': 'simple'})

@app.route('/slow')
@cache.cached(timeout=60)
def slow_function():
    import time
    time.sleep(5)  # Simulate a slow response
    return "This is a cached response"
```

## Explanation:

- The @cache.cached(timeout=60) decorator caches the response of the slow_function endpoint for 60 seconds. This way, subsequent requests within 60 seconds return almost instantly without recomputing the response.

Caching with Redis

Using **Redis** as a cache backend can further enhance performance, especially in distributed environments:

**Installation**:

```
pip install redis Flask-Caching
```

**Configuration**:

```
app.config['CACHE_TYPE'] = 'RedisCache'
app.config['CACHE_REDIS_URL'] = 'redis://localhost:6379/0'
cache = Cache(app)
```

**Redis** caches data in memory, making it extremely fast for retrieving frequently requested data, such as product lists or user profiles.

3. Database Optimization

**Database performance** is often a significant factor in API latency. Here are some strategies to optimize database queries:

3.1 Query Optimization

- **Use Indexes**: Adding indexes to columns that are frequently queried can significantly improve query performance.
- **Avoid N+1 Query Problems**: The N+1 query problem occurs when the API makes one initial query to retrieve records and then makes additional queries for each record. Use **SQLAlchemy's joinedload()** to load related data in a single query.

```
from sqlalchemy.orm import joinedload

users = session.query(User).options(joinedload(User.posts)).all()
```

3.2 Connection Pooling

Connection pooling helps manage database connections efficiently by maintaining a pool of connections that can be reused, rather than creating a new one for every request.

- **SQLAlchemy Connection Pooling**:

```
from sqlalchemy import create_engine

engine = create_engine(
    'postgresql://user:password@localhost/dbname',
    pool_size=10,
    max_overflow=20,
    pool_timeout=30
)
```

3.3 Using Read Replicas

If you are handling a large volume of read requests, consider setting up **read replicas**. You can configure your Flask API to use the primary database for writes and read replicas for reading.

4. Asynchronous and Batch Processing

Handling API requests asynchronously can significantly improve performance, especially when dealing with I/O-bound operations.

4.1 Async Routes with Quart

Use **Quart**, an asynchronous variant of Flask, to create non-blocking routes that can handle more concurrent requests.

```
from quart import Quart
import asyncio

app = Quart(__name__)

@app.route('/async')
async def async_route():
    await asyncio.sleep(3)
    return {"message": "Async response"}
```

4.2 Batch Processing

Instead of processing each request individually, consider batching operations. For example, if a client needs to create multiple resources, provide a batch API that processes all the requests in a single transaction.

```
@app.route('/batch_create_users', methods=['POST'])
def batch_create_users():
    users_data = request.get_json()
    for user_data in users_data:
        # Process each user creation
        pass
    return jsonify({"message": "Users created"}), 201
```

5. Content Compression

Reducing the size of responses helps decrease the time required to send data over the network, which in turn reduces response times. **Gzip** is a popular compression format used to compress HTTP responses.

Using Flask-Compress

**Installation**:

```
pip install Flask-Compress
```

**Setup**:

```
from flask import Flask
from flask_compress import Compress

app = Flask(__name__)
Compress(app)

@app.route('/large')
def large_response():
    return "This is a large response" * 1000
```

**Flask-Compress** will compress the response automatically, reducing its size and speeding up the transfer.

6. Minimizing Middleware and Bottlenecks

Middleware adds processing time to each request, so you should minimize unnecessary middleware to reduce latency. Focus on lightweight, efficient middleware that does not block the request path.

- **Remove Unused Middleware**: Audit your middleware stack regularly and remove any unused or unnecessary components.
- **Avoid Blocking Operations**: Middleware that involves synchronous I/O, such as reading from disk or external APIs, should be avoided or made asynchronous.

7. Rate Limiting

**Rate limiting** is a technique used to control the number of requests a user or client can make in a given time frame. Rate limiting helps prevent abuse, such as DDoS attacks, and ensures that resources are available for all users.

Using Flask-Limiter

**Installation**:

```
pip install Flask-Limiter
```

**Setup**:

```
from flask import Flask
from flask_limiter import Limiter

app = Flask(__name__)
limiter = Limiter(app, key_func=lambda: request.remote_addr)

@app.route('/limited')
@limiter.limit("5 per minute")
def limited_route():
    return "This route is rate limited"
```

**Explanation**:

- The @limiter.limit("5 per minute") decorator limits access to the route to 5 requests per minute per IP address. Rate limiting helps manage traffic and prevent abuse.

8. Load Testing and Scaling

Load testing helps you understand how your API behaves under different traffic loads. It enables you to identify potential bottlenecks and scale accordingly.

Load Testing Tools

- **Apache JMeter**: A powerful tool for load testing and measuring performance under various conditions.
- **Locust**: An open-source load testing tool that allows you to simulate concurrent users and measure API performance.

Scaling Strategies

1. **Vertical Scaling**: Increase the capacity of the server by adding more CPU or memory. This is straightforward but has limits.
2. **Horizontal Scaling**: Add more instances of your API server to distribute traffic across multiple machines. This can be achieved using load balancers like **NGINX** or cloud-based load balancers (e.g., **AWS ELB**).

Using a Load Balancer

**Load balancers** distribute incoming requests across multiple instances, reducing the load on any single instance.

- **NGINX**: Configure NGINX as a reverse proxy to distribute requests to multiple Flask instances running on different ports or servers.
- **Cloud Load Balancers**: AWS, Azure, and Google Cloud provide built-in load balancers that can automatically scale your application in response to changing traffic demands.

9. Best Practices for API Optimization

- **Keep Responses Lightweight**: Minimize the amount of data in your responses by excluding unnecessary fields and using pagination.
- **Use HTTP/2**: HTTP/2 provides improved speed and efficiency for serving multiple requests and responses concurrently.
- **Avoid Unnecessary Work in Endpoints**: Avoid putting complex business logic in your API routes. Move these to background workers if they don't need to be handled synchronously.
- **Leverage Client-Side Caching**: Set appropriate cache headers (Cache-Control, ETag) to allow clients to cache responses, reducing the need for repeated server requests.

# Deploying Flask APIs

O nce you've built and optimized your Flask API, the next step is to deploy it to a production environment. Deploying involves setting up a hosting platform, configuring a web server, implementing security measures, and setting up continuous integration and deployment (CI/CD) pipelines. In this chapter, we'll explore different deployment strategies, hosting options, and best practices for making your Flask API accessible to the world.

1. Choosing a Hosting Platform

The first step in deploying a Flask API is selecting a suitable hosting platform. Different platforms offer varying levels of control, scalability, and pricing. Here are some common options:

- **Cloud Platforms**: AWS, Google Cloud, Azure
- **Platform-as-a-Service (PaaS)**: Heroku, DigitalOcean App Platform
- **Virtual Private Server (VPS)**: DigitalOcean, Linode, Vultr
- **Container Platforms**: Docker, Kubernetes, AWS ECS, Google Kubernetes Engine (GKE)

2. Deploying with WSGI and a Web Server

Flask's built-in development server is not suitable for production. Instead, you should deploy your Flask app using a WSGI server like **Gunicorn** or **uWSGI** combined with a web server like **NGINX** or **Apache**. This combination allows for efficient handling of incoming requests.

2.1 Using Gunicorn with NGINX

**Gunicorn** is a popular WSGI server that is simple to set up and works well with Flask.

**Installing Gunicorn**:

```
pip install gunicorn
```

**Running Your Flask App with Gunicorn**:

```
gunicorn -w 4 -b 0.0.0.0:8000 app:app
```

**Explanation**: The -w 4 flag specifies 4 worker processes. Adjust this number based on your server's CPU cores.

**Setting Up NGINX as a Reverse Proxy**:

**NGINX** acts as a reverse proxy that forwards requests to Gunicorn. Install and configure NGINX as follows:

- **Install NGINX**:

```
sudo apt-get install nginx
```

- **Configure NGINX** by editing the configuration file (e.g., /etc/nginx/sites-available/default):

```
server {
    listen 80;
    server_name your-domain.com;

    location / {
```

```
        proxy_pass http://127.0.0.1:8000;
        proxy_set_header Host $host;
        proxy_set_header X-Real-IP $remote_addr;
        proxy_set_header X-Forwarded-For
        $proxy_add_x_forwarded_for;
        proxy_set_header X-Forwarded-Proto $scheme;
    }
}
```

- **Restart NGINX**:

```
sudo systemctl restart nginx
```

## 2.2 Deploying with Docker

**Docker** allows you to package your Flask API along with all its dependencies into a container that can run consistently on different environments.

### Create a Dockerfile:

```
# Use the official Python image as the base image
FROM python:3.9-slim

# Set the working directory
WORKDIR /app

# Copy the requirements file and install dependencies
COPY requirements.txt requirements.txt
RUN pip install -r requirements.txt

# Copy the rest of the application code
COPY . .

# Expose the port the app runs on
EXPOSE 8000
```

```
# Command to run the app with Gunicorn
CMD ["gunicorn", "-w", "4", "-b", "0.0.0.0:8000", "app:app"]
```

**Build the Docker Image**:

```
docker build -t flask-api .
```

**Run the Docker Container**:

```
docker run -p 8000:8000 flask-api
```

**Deploying with Docker Compose**: Create a docker-compose.yml file to define multiple services (such as your app and database) and manage them with a single command.

```
version: '3'
services:
  web:
    build: .
    ports:
      - "8000:8000"
    depends_on:
      - db

  db:
    image: postgres:13
    environment:
      POSTGRES_USER: user
      POSTGRES_PASSWORD: password
      POSTGRES_DB: mydb
```

**Explanation**: This setup defines two services: web (your Flask API) and db (a PostgreSQL database). The depends_on option ensures that the database starts before the API.

3. Continuous Integration and Deployment (CI/CD)

Setting up a **CI/CD pipeline** automates the process of testing, building, and deploying your Flask API. This reduces the chances of human error and speeds up the deployment process.

3.1 CI/CD with GitHub Actions

**GitHub Actions** is a popular CI/CD tool that integrates directly with your GitHub repository.

**Create a Workflow File** in .github/workflows/deploy.yml:

```
name: Deploy to Server

on:
  push:
    branches:
      - main

jobs:
  deploy:
    runs-on: ubuntu-latest

    steps:
    - name: Check out code
      uses: actions/checkout@v2

    - name: Set up Python
      uses: actions/setup-python@v2
      with:
        python-version: '3.9'

    - name: Install dependencies
      run: |
        pip install -r requirements.txt

    - name: Run tests
      run: |
        pytest
```

```
- name: Deploy via SSH
  uses: appleboy/ssh-action@master
  with:
    host: ${{ secrets.SERVER_IP }}
    username: ${{ secrets.SERVER_USER }}
    password: ${{ secrets.SERVER_PASSWORD }}
    script: |
      cd /var/www/your-app
      git pull origin main
      sudo systemctl restart gunicorn
```

**Explanation**:

- The workflow triggers on a push to the main branch.
- It installs dependencies, runs tests, and connects to your server via SSH to pull the latest code and restart Gunicorn.

3.2 Automating with Docker and Kubernetes

For more advanced deployments, you can use **Kubernetes** to orchestrate your Docker containers. Kubernetes automates deployment, scaling, and management of containerized applications.

**Create a Kubernetes Deployment**:

```
apiVersion: apps/v1
kind: Deployment
metadata:
  name: flask-api
spec:
  replicas: 3
  selector:
    matchLabels:
      app: flask-api
  template:
    metadata:
```

```
  labels:
    app: flask-api
spec:
  containers:
  - name: flask-api
    image: flask-api:latest
    ports:
    - containerPort: 8000
```

## Deploy with kubectl:

```
kubectl apply -f deployment.yaml
```

## Expose the Deployment:

```
kubectl expose deployment flask-api --type=LoadBalancer --port=80
--target-port=8000
```

4. Securing Your Flask API

Security is a critical aspect of any deployment. Here are some best practices to secure your Flask API:

1. **Use HTTPS**: Encrypt traffic between clients and your server using **SSL/TLS** certificates. You can obtain free SSL certificates from **Let's Encrypt**.
2. **Set Up a Firewall**: Configure a firewall to restrict access to critical services and only allow necessary traffic through specific ports.
3. **Implement Authentication and Authorization**: Use **JWT** or **OAuth** to secure your API endpoints and protect sensitive data.
4. **Limit User Input**: Sanitize and validate user input to prevent **SQL injection, cross-site scripting (XSS)**, and other attacks.
5. **Regular Backups**: Regularly back up your database and application code to ensure you can recover from data loss or corruption.

## 5. Load Balancing and Scaling

As your application grows, you may need to scale it to handle increased traffic. Load balancing helps distribute incoming requests across multiple instances of your API, improving reliability and performance.

### 5.1 Using NGINX as a Load Balancer

NGINX can act as a load balancer to distribute traffic to multiple instances of your Flask API running on different servers or ports.

```
upstream flask_app {
    server 127.0.0.1:8000;
    server 127.0.0.1:8001;
    server 127.0.0.1:8002;
}

server {
    listen 80;
    server_name your-domain.com;

    location / {
        proxy_pass http://flask_app;
        proxy_set_header Host $host;
        proxy_set_header X-Real-IP $remote_addr;
        proxy_set_header X-Forwarded-For
$proxy_add_x_forwarded_for;
        proxy_set_header X-Forwarded-Proto $scheme;
    }
}
```

### 5.2 Auto-Scaling with Kubernetes

Kubernetes can automatically scale your application based on CPU or memory usage. You can configure **Horizontal Pod Autoscaler (HPA)** to manage auto-scaling.

```
kubectl autoscale deployment flask-api --min=2 --max=10
--cpu-percent=70
```

# Advanced Topics in API Development

Building robust APIs involves more than just handling basic CRUD operations. As your application grows, you may need to implement advanced features that enhance your API's capabilities, efficiency, and flexibility. These features can include real-time data, WebSockets, GraphQL integration, and implementing third-party authentication.

In this chapter, you'll learn about several advanced topics in API development that can help you take your Flask-based APIs to the next level.

1. Implementing WebSockets for Real-Time Communication

WebSockets enable real-time, bidirectional communication between the server and clients. Unlike traditional HTTP, which follows a request-response model, WebSockets allow persistent connections where the server can push updates to clients as needed.

Using Flask-SocketIO

**Flask-SocketIO** is an extension for Flask that enables WebSocket communication using the **Socket.IO** protocol.

**Installing Flask-SocketIO**:

```
pip install flask-socketio
```

**Setting Up Flask-SocketIO**:

```python
from flask import Flask, render_template
from flask_socketio import SocketIO, emit

app = Flask(__name__)
app.config['SECRET_KEY'] = 'secret!'
socketio = SocketIO(app)

@app.route('/')
def index():
    return render_template('index.html')

@socketio.on('message')
def handle_message(message):
    print('received message: ' + message)
    emit('response', {'data': 'Message received!'})

if __name__ == '__main__':
    socketio.run(app, debug=True)
```

## Explanation:

- The @socketio.on('message') decorator listens for messages from clients and emits a response back to the client.
- You can handle other events like connecting, disconnecting, and custom events.

**Creating a Client-Side WebSocket**: In your HTML file (templates/index.html), include the Socket.IO client library and set up a connection:

```html
<!DOCTYPE html>
<html>
<head>
    <script
    src="https://cdn.socket.io/4.0.0/socket.io.min.js"></script>
    <script type="text/javascript">
        var socket = io();
```

```
        socket.on('connect', function() {
            socket.send('Hello from client');
        });
        socket.on('response', function(data) {
            console.log(data);
        });
    </script>
</head>
<body>
    <h1>WebSocket Example</h1>
</body>
</html>
```

**Testing WebSocket Communication**: Run the Flask app and open the HTML file in a browser. You should see a connection established and messages being exchanged between the client and server.

2. Integrating GraphQL with Flask

**GraphQL** is a query language for APIs that allows clients to request only the data they need, making APIs more flexible and efficient. It contrasts with REST's fixed endpoints and rigid responses.

Using Flask-GraphQL

**Installing Flask-GraphQL**:

```
pip install flask-graphql graphene
```

**Creating a Basic GraphQL Schema**: Define a GraphQL schema using **Graphene**:

```
import graphene
from flask import Flask
from flask_graphql import GraphQLView

class User(graphene.ObjectType):
```

```
    id = graphene.ID()
    username = graphene.String()
    email = graphene.String()

class Query(graphene.ObjectType):
    users = graphene.List(User)

    def resolve_users(self, info):
        return [
            User(id=1, username="Alice",
            email="alice@example.com"),
            User(id=2, username="Bob", email="bob@example.com")
        ]

schema = graphene.Schema(query=Query)

app = Flask(__name__)
app.add_url_rule('/graphql',
view_func=GraphQLView.as_view('graphql', schema=schema,
graphiql=True))

if __name__ == '__main__':
    app.run(debug=True)
```

**Explanation**:

- The Query class defines a query type with a users field that returns a list of users.
- The resolve_users method returns sample user data.
- The GraphQLView adds a /graphql endpoint with the interactive **GraphiQL** interface enabled.

**Testing the GraphQL Endpoint**: Visit http://localhost:5000/graphql to access the **GraphiQL** interface. You can test queries like:

```
{
  users {
    id
    username
    email
  }
}
```

## 3. Implementing OAuth Authentication

OAuth allows users to authenticate with third-party services like Google, Facebook, or GitHub. This method is secure and reduces the need for managing user credentials directly.

Using Flask-Dance for OAuth

**Flask-Dance** is an extension that simplifies integrating OAuth with Flask.

- **Installing Flask-Dance**:

```
pip install Flask-Dance
```

- **Setting Up Google OAuth**: Register your application in the **Google Developer Console** to obtain a **Client ID** and **Client Secret**.
- **Configuring Flask-Dance**:

```
from flask import Flask, redirect, url_for
from flask_dance.contrib.google import make_google_blueprint,
google

app = Flask(__name__)
app.secret_key = "supersecretkey"
google_bp = make_google_blueprint(client_id="your-client-id",
client_secret="your-client-secret", redirect_to="google_login")
app.register_blueprint(google_bp, url_prefix="/login")
```

```
@app.route('/')
def index():
    if not google.authorized:
        return redirect(url_for("google.login"))
    resp = google.get("/plus/v1/people/me")
    assert resp.ok, resp.text
    return f"You are {resp.json()['displayName']}"

if __name__ == '__main__':
    app.run(debug=True)
```

**Explanation**:

- The make_google_blueprint function sets up a Google OAuth blueprint.
- The / route checks if the user is authenticated with Google. If not, it redirects them to the Google login page.

4. Implementing Rate Limiting and Security Measures

As your API grows, security becomes increasingly important. **Rate limiting** protects your API from abuse, and other security measures help prevent common attacks like **SQL Injection, Cross-Site Scripting (XSS)**, and **Cross-Site Request Forgery (CSRF)**.

Using Flask-Limiter for Rate Limiting

**Installing Flask-Limiter**:

```
pip install Flask-Limiter
```

**Setting Up Rate Limiting**:

```
from flask import Flask
from flask_limiter import Limiter

app = Flask(__name__)
```

```
limiter = Limiter(app, key_func=lambda: request.remote_addr)

@app.route('/api/resource')
@limiter.limit("10 per minute")
def limited_route():
    return "This route is rate limited"
```

### Explanation:

- The @limiter.limit("10 per minute") decorator limits access to 10 requests per minute per IP address.

5. Extending APIs with Background Tasks

Sometimes, API endpoints need to perform long-running tasks like sending emails, generating reports, or processing files. These tasks should be handled asynchronously to avoid blocking requests.

Using Celery for Background Tasks

### Installing Celery:

```
pip install celery redis
```

### Configuring Celery:

```
from celery import Celery

def make_celery(app):
    celery = Celery(
        app.import_name,
        backend=app.config['CELERY_RESULT_BACKEND'],
        broker=app.config['CELERY_BROKER_URL']
    )
    celery.conf.update(app.config)
    return celery
```

```
app = Flask(__name__)
app.config.update(
    CELERY_BROKER_URL='redis://localhost:6379/0',
    CELERY_RESULT_BACKEND='redis://localhost:6379/0'
)

celery = make_celery(app)
```

## Defining and Triggering Background Tasks:

```
@celery.task
def send_email(email, message):
    print(f"Sending email to {email}: {message}")

@app.route('/send', methods=['POST'])
def send_route():
    data = request.get_json()
    send_email.delay(data['email'], data['message'])
    return jsonify({"message": "Email sent"}), 202
```

6. Supporting Internationalization and Localization

Internationalization (i18n) allows your API to support multiple languages and regional formats, while localization (l10n) adapts it to specific regions or languages.

Using Flask-Babel for i18n

## Installing Flask-Babel:

```
pip install Flask-Babel
```

## Setting Up Flask-Babel:

```
from flask import Flask
from flask_babel import Babel

app = Flask(__name__)
```

```
app.config['BABEL_DEFAULT_LOCALE'] = 'en'
babel = Babel(app)

@babel.localeselector
def get_locale():
    return request.accept_languages.best_match(['en', 'es', 'fr'])

@app.route('/greet')
def greet():
    return gettext("Hello, World!")
```

## Explanation:

- The @babel.localeselector decorator determines the best language match for each request.
- Use gettext to mark translatable strings.

# Practical Projects

T he best way to solidify your understanding of API development concepts is through practical projects. Building real-world applications will allow you to apply everything you've learned, identify gaps in your knowledge, and gain experience working through challenges.

In this chapter, we'll outline a series of practical projects of increasing complexity that you can build using Flask. Each project is designed to reinforce different aspects of API development, from simple CRUD operations to real-time features, third-party integrations, and scalability.

Project 1: Task Management API

**Overview**: Build a task management API where users can create, read, update, and delete tasks. This project focuses on implementing basic CRUD operations, authentication, and authorization.

**Key Features**:

- **CRUD** operations for managing tasks (Create, Read, Update, Delete).
- **User authentication** with JWT.
- **Role-based access control** (users can only manage their own tasks).

**Skills Reinforced**:

- Database modeling with SQLAlchemy.
- User authentication and JWT handling.

- RESTful API design principles.

**Project Breakdown**:

1. **User Authentication**: Implement user registration and login with JWT-based authentication.
2. **Task Endpoints**: Create CRUD endpoints for tasks, ensuring that each user can only manage their own tasks.
3. **User Roles and Permissions**: Add a role-based authorization feature (e.g., admin vs. regular user).

Project 2: Real-Time Chat Application

**Overview**: Create a real-time chat application using Flask-SocketIO. This project will help you understand how to use WebSockets to build applications that require real-time communication.

**Key Features**:

- **User-to-user messaging**.
- **WebSocket-based real-time communication** using Flask-SocketIO.
- **Message persistence** in a database.

**Skills Reinforced**:

- WebSocket communication.
- Frontend and backend integration.
- Asynchronous communication handling.

**Project Breakdown**:

1. **Setting Up WebSocket Communication**: Use Flask-SocketIO to set up WebSocket communication between users.
2. **Message Storage**: Save chat messages to a database and retrieve them when users reconnect.

3. **Frontend Integration**: Use HTML and JavaScript to create a simple chat interface that connects to your WebSocket server.

Project 3: Weather Forecast API with External Integrations

**Overview**: Build an API that provides weather information by integrating a third-party weather service like OpenWeatherMap. This project focuses on external API integration and data manipulation.

**Key Features**:

- **Weather data retrieval** using a third-party API.
- **Caching of responses** to minimize redundant API calls.
- **Error handling** for external API requests.

**Skills Reinforced**:

- Integrating external APIs.
- Handling API errors and timeouts.
- Implementing caching mechanisms.

**Project Breakdown**:

1. **Weather Data Endpoint**: Create an endpoint that fetches weather data based on city or GPS coordinates.
2. **Caching**: Implement caching using Flask-Caching or Redis to avoid redundant calls to the external weather API.
3. **Error Handling**: Gracefully handle errors like API downtime or incorrect API keys.

Project 4: E-Commerce Product Catalog API

**Overview**: Develop a product catalog API for an e-commerce application. This project will introduce more complex data relationships and pagination, essential skills for real-world applications.

**Key Features**:

- **Product management**: CRUD operations for products, categories, and brands.
- **Pagination and filtering** for products.
- **User authentication** and authorization (e.g., admin users can manage products, regular users can view them).

**Skills Reinforced**:

- Modeling complex relationships with SQLAlchemy.
- Implementing pagination and filtering.
- Managing user roles and permissions.

**Project Breakdown**:

1. **Product Management**: Set up CRUD operations for managing products, with models for categories and brands.
2. **User Authentication**: Allow admins to create and update products, while regular users can only view them.
3. **Pagination and Filtering**: Add pagination to product listings and filtering by category or brand.

Project 5: Online Voting and Polls API

**Overview**: Create an online voting system where users can create polls and vote on them. This project will demonstrate working with relational data and handling constraints like preventing duplicate votes.

**Key Features**:

- **Poll creation and management**.
- **Voting restrictions** to prevent duplicate voting.
- **Real-time poll results** using WebSockets.

**Skills Reinforced**:

- Implementing relational models with SQLAlchemy.
- Creating custom validation logic for voting constraints.
- Real-time data updates.

**Project Breakdown**:

1. **Poll and Option Models**: Create models for polls and options using SQLAlchemy.
2. **Vote Validation**: Ensure that users can only vote once per poll.
3. **Real-Time Poll Results**: Use Flask-SocketIO to provide real-time updates of poll results.

Project 6: Fitness Tracker API with User Goals

**Overview**: Build a fitness tracking API where users can log their workouts, track progress, and set fitness goals. This project will cover more complex data interactions and user-specific data tracking.

**Key Features**:

- **Workout logging** and history tracking.
- **User-specific goals** and progress monitoring.
- **Data analytics and summary endpoints** for users to track their progress.

**Skills Reinforced**:

- Managing user-specific data.
- Data aggregation and reporting.
- User-specific authorization.

**Project Breakdown**:

1. **Workout Logging**: Allow users to log workouts and track their daily or weekly exercise.

2. **Setting Goals**: Create endpoints for users to set and update fitness goals.
3. **Progress Reports**: Implement summary endpoints that provide users with progress reports and analytics.

Project 7: Blog and Commenting Platform

**Overview**: Create a blog API where users can create, read, update, and delete posts, and other users can comment on them. This project involves managing nested data and creating a social interaction feature.

**Key Features**:

- **Blog post creation and management**.
- **Nested comments** and replies.
- **User authentication** and role-based authorization.

**Skills Reinforced**:

- Working with nested data structures.
- Handling complex authorization scenarios.
- Implementing features that involve multiple user interactions.

**Project Breakdown**:

1. **Blog Post Management**: Set up endpoints for creating and managing blog posts.
2. **Commenting System**: Allow users to comment on blog posts and reply to other comments.
3. **Admin Authorization**: Implement role-based access control for post and comment moderation.

Project 8: API for an Online Marketplace

**Overview**: Develop an API for an online marketplace where users can list items for sale, search for products, and purchase items. This project covers complex user interactions, payment integrations, and product management.

**Key Features**:

- **Product listing and search**.
- **User-to-user transactions**.
- **Integration with a payment gateway**.

**Skills Reinforced**:

- Complex user interactions and data relationships.
- Payment gateway integration.
- Secure transaction handling.

**Project Breakdown**:

1. **Product Listings**: Allow users to create and manage product listings.
2. **Search and Filters**: Implement search and filtering capabilities for users to find products.
3. **Payment Integration**: Integrate with a payment gateway like Stripe or PayPal for handling transactions.

www.ingramcontent.com/pod-product-compliance
Lightning Source LLC
LaVergne TN
LVHW051702050326
832903LV00032B/3957